Claude-Maria Vadrot
Victoria Ivleva

RUSSIA
TODAY

From Holy Russia to Perestroika

atomium books

To Sophie-Leila,
so that she may also get to know the Russians.

First published in the United States 1990 by

    Atomium Books Inc.
    Suite 300
    1013 Centre Road
    Wilmington, DE 19805.

First published, in French, by Editions du May, Paris, 1988
under the title "Temps Presents de la Russie".
Text and pictures copyright © Editions du May 1988.
Translation copyright © Atomium Books 1990.
All rights reserved. No part of this publication may be reproduced,
stored in a retrieval system, or transmitted, in any form or by any
means, electronic, mechanical, photocopying, recording, or otherwise,
without the prior permission of Editions du May.

Printed in France and bound in Belgium by Color Print Graphix.
Translation of English text by Harry Swalef.
Editing of English text by Linda Bernier.

First U.S. Edition
2 4 6 8 10 9 7 5 3 1

RUSSIA
TODAY

PREFACE

Since 1985 the Soviet Union has experienced a period of upheaval unprecedented in its turbulent history. The seventieth anniversary of the Socialist regime, in November 1987, was marked by traumatic change. Emanating from the Kremlin, Mikhail Gorbachev's earth-shaking reforms are gradually being felt throughout the immense country of 285 million people. The revolution of the 1980s does not enjoy unanimous support any more than that of 1917 did. Within the one-party state, Leninist revivalists have found their own "White Army" to support them: Russian conservatism. With his roots ensconced in religion and Slavophile traditions, the Russian conservative has always maintained his country as the center of the world and is determined to safeguard its purity and truths from foreign influences. From Peter the Great, who horrified his compatriots as the first tsar to travel abroad, to Raissa Gorbachev, flaunting her own distinctive elegance at Paris fashion shows, Russian conservatism manifests the same audacity, defiance and rejection when dealing with those things foreign to Mother Russia.

Despite seventy years of effort, the country has not forgotten a history that still molds people's behavior and rejection of each other. Those who believe that the USSR is no longer Russia don't really understand the country. It's like forgetting that all Soviets are not Russian, and that millions of them hardly understand the language of the Russian unifiers.

During these times of political, social, economic, and cultural turmoil, the present and future of the country have never before been so intimately linked with the past. This is a continent where notions and realities constantly clash. Here, light years seem to separate space-age rockets from the peasants who, twenty-five miles outside Moscow, still have no running water. The Kirghiz, in the south of the country, still live in contented pastoral tranquility, roaming the Pamir mountains. Except in their cities, they are hardly aware of this Russian Socialism business, with its meddlesome complexities and zeal.

The time is propitious for a fresh look at this seemingly unfathomable empire. The West is intrigued, uneasy, surprised, sceptical and

PREFACE

fascinated. Prisoners of their entrenched reflexes, Westerners are beginning to ask countless questions about this country which is undergoing such intense internal tension. Because it is also a time when the USSR is opening up to journalistic investigation, a Soviet photographer and a French reporter have combined their thoughts and impressions to present a unique look at life in the Soviet Union today. This book, which is the result of several months of travel throughout the country, was produced in complete and unprecedented freedom. After the authorities gave their permission to do the book, they did not exercise any control over the text or photographs.

Victoria Ivleva, one of the Soviet Union's leading professional photographers, has thus been able to explore her country with me. Her photographs, supplemented by my own, lay bare the most secret aspects of Russian life. She has guided me toward a better understanding of a country I have frequently visited over many years. It's a country I love, despite its differences, excesses and difficulties in shedding outdated notions and reflexes. These have been conditioned by decades of sailing on the wrong course and cannot be corrected in just a few years with Gorbachev at the helm.

This sympathetic, but not flattering, account is the synthesis of our surprises, fears, concerns and past experiences. Being Soviet or not makes a difference in the way one feels about this immense country which has been stagnating for years on the periphery of the world. Even though I've been to the Soviet Union many times, I was just visiting. Victoria, however, was born in Leningrad and lives in Moscow. Our experiences, therefore, are not the same. What surprises or amuses one, may leave the other completely cold or sceptical.

In this book we wanted to capture the Soviet Union's amazing current history without neglecting the eternal images of Russia. We have tried to show everything that's changing as well as the duality and diversity of this country-continent. Of course, it's impossible to say everything there is to say and show everything there is to show in such an endeavor. Our intention, first and foremost, was to get people interested in knowing and understanding the country, and to show how thin the Iron Curtain has worn, so much so that it will soon, perhaps, be nothing but a bad memory.

PREFACE

Be it Moscow, Leningrad, Tallinn, Tbilisi or the lost villages of the Russian *taïga* (forest), the duality and contradictions of Soviet life exist all over the country. We have selected stories and images to illustrate the things that shock and change and those that have remained the same through the ages — from the pious men of Ulyanovsk to the Moscow fashion designer Slava Zaytsev, via the punks of Leningrad, the fishermen of Sakhalin, the emerging world of private business and restaurants, the peasants of Georgia, the rearguard and avant-garde artists, the uniformed schoolchildren, the Jews, the Muslims, the Baptists, the wooden *isbas*, the first traffic jams, the disintegrating Communist Party, the demonstrations, the cold, the snow, and the many town markets where women wear themselves out in search of the products they need. It's a country where cultures clash and cohabitate.

There are also pictures of everyday life, street scenes and images of people at work, enjoying themselves, praying, eating, shopping and just going about their lives like people everywhere. And there are unique and rare pictures, never seen before, that we have uncovered behind the enduring cliches. They provide stark and sometimes astounding insights into the Soviet Union, whose image, for many, is merely the red walls of the Kremlin. That is like thinking the United States adds up to nothing more than the White House, the skyscrapers of Manhattan, the glamour of Hollywood, and a meal of hamburgers and Coke.

This journey is also an impressionistic chronicle of *perestroika* and *glasnost*, the battle cries of Mikhail Gorbachev in his struggle to effect change and bring the Soviet people to terms with their past — from the bloody tyranny of Stalin, who massacred millions to establish his regime, to the harsh stagnation of Leonid Brezhnev, who led his country to the brink of economic and social disaster.

These are images and tales that illustrate to what extent the USSR is striving, at times successfully, to resemble the West, and to what extent, it, fortunately, remains different.

Claude-Marie Vadrot

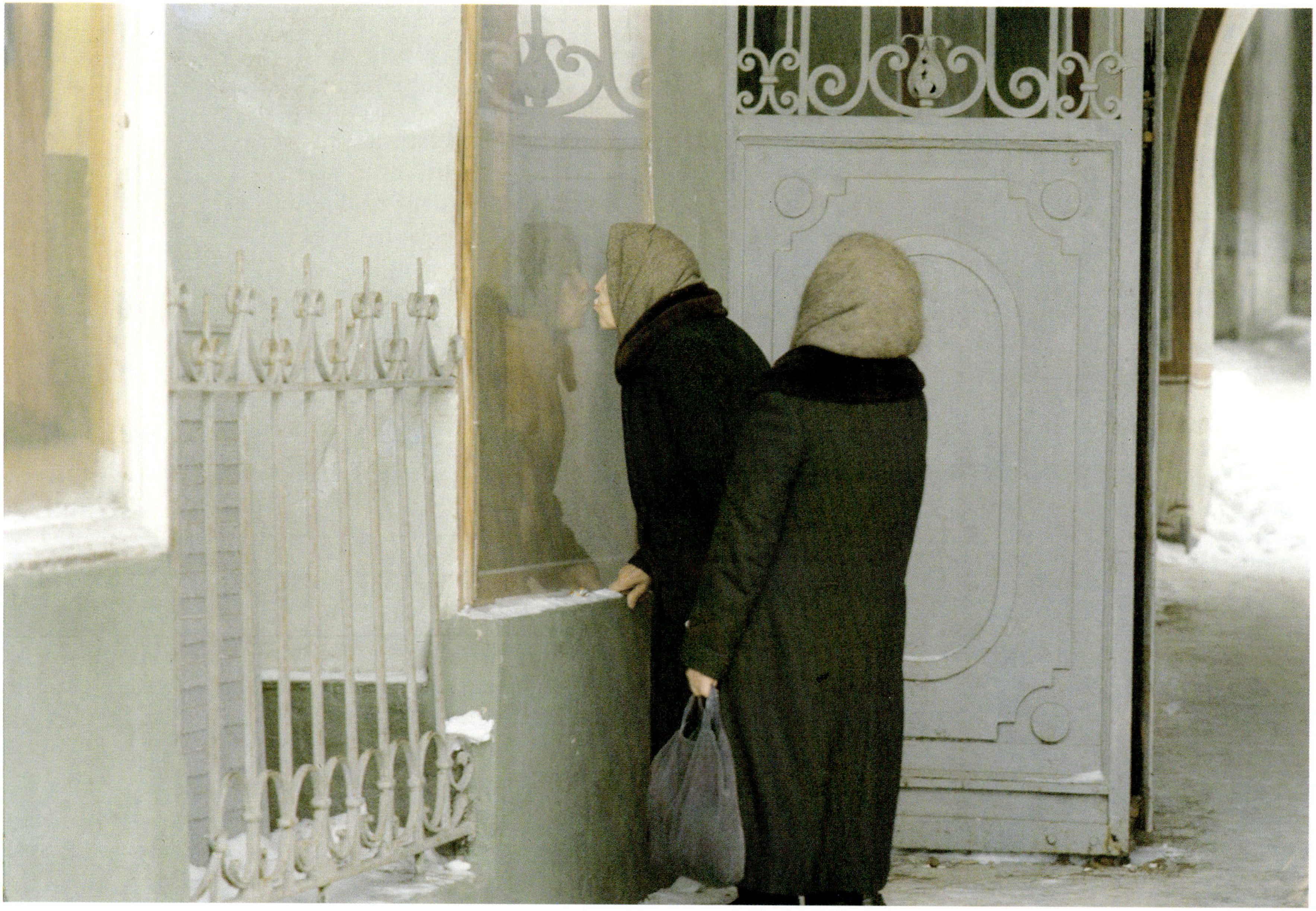

RELIGION

In the year of grace 988, when he baptized the first Russ inhabiting the Dnieper basin, the prince and future saint, Vladimir of Kiev, was about as far from sanctity as one could be. Born out of wedlock, his father was a Varangian from Scandinavia and his mother a Slav maid servant. He belonged to that handful of men from the north who came to govern the Slav peoples in the ninth century. After assassinating his brother, he was brought to power by the Slavs. Most of them were still pagan at the time, despite the efforts of Cyril, the monk who had come to preach the gospel in the Crimea around 860. To help spread the Christian creed of Byzantium in the Slavonic language, Cyril invented an alphabet inspired by the one used by the Greeks. His efforts, however, were not sufficient to shake their primitive convictions. Though scattered from the Black Sea to the Gulf of Finland, the Slavs were beginning to regard themselves as a nation.

The Varagians, who ruled over the Slavs, devoted so much time to ferociously fighting for power that they contributed to the fragmentation of the Kievan state.

After many fierce battles against the sovereigns and armies of the Byzantine Empire, Prince Vladimir decided to embrace their faith, primarily so he could marry Anne, the sister of the Byzantine emperor. The emperor had refused to give the beautiful Christian maiden to a barbarian, even for sound political reasons. Once converted, Prince Vladimir declared that what was good for him was good for his people, so they were firmly enjoined to immerse themselves in the Dnieper for a collective baptism, which lasted several days. Thus, the Russ, soon to become the Russians, made their entry into Christendom.

The new faith spread rapidly throughout the realm. Only Novgorod and some rural areas long resisted this evangelization conducted under

IN THE ZAGORSK MONASTERY

Forty-five miles from Moscow, the monastery, seminary, and churches of Zagorsk form one of the active centers of Orthodoxy.
The recent symbolic return of the Patriarch to Moscow will not affect the immutable "pious way," the traditional journey of the faithful who come to Zagorsk to kiss the holiest icons of the country.
As elsewhere, the icons have been under glass for years, a protective measure against these passionate expressions of faith. During the time of militant atheism such practices were said to spread disease.

RELIGION

the stern direction of Greek priests and prelates. Christianity helped strengthen the nascent national sentiment of the Slavs as they gradually merged with the ruling minority, the Varangians. However this religion, with its highly formalized and emotionally appealing rituals, did not bring political stability to the land. Disorder and division reigned, except in Novgorod, a city of traders, which had become a small republic desperately determined to safeguard its autonomy.

Until the arrival of the Tatars in 1249 some fifty princes ruled Kiev. The last one was Alexander Nevsky. During the long period of Tatar domination "Russia" managed to maintain its autonomy, although its center shifted to Suzdal. The Metropolitan (the chief bishop in a province), who was Greek and Orthodox, remained in Kiev. The Russians followed the Christians of Byzantium in the schism with Rome in 1054, and began to consider all other Christians non-believers.

Paganism was on the decline at this time, even though it left its mark on many village practices and beliefs. It was during this period that the peasants began setting aside a *krasny ugol* (red or beautiful corner) in their *isbas*. There they set up their icons, burned candles, and prayed, mostly on Saturday evenings. Their beliefs were still mixed, and they worshipped both God and nature. These Orthodox peasants already knew how to practice their faith without popes (priests in the Orthodox Church). Centuries later Old Believers, fleeing the persecution of tsars, or Orthodox believers, persecuted by Communism, still managed to pray without popes. In this way they perpetuated certain rites linked with nature and venerated saints as if they were gods. In the thirteenth and fourteenth centuries the Church imposed its authority on the land and its inhabitants. The monasteries expanded their holdings and recruited peasants, promising them paradise and, above all, tax privileges.

Moscow, which had become the capital of the Russian principality after the death of Alexander Nevsky in the thirteenth century, became the capital of Russian Orthodoxy when the Metropolitan moved there in 1330. When in 1448 the rulers ousted the Greek Metropolitan and replaced him with a Russian, the Russian Orthodox Church became truly Russian. Thus, all the elements of Russian political and religious history were in place, setting the stage for all the drama and conflict that would evolve between the Church and the emerging State.

RELIGION

It was Ivan III, known as Ivan the Great, who, with the support of the Church, strengthened the Muscovite State from 1462 to the beginning of the 16th century. He subdued Novgorod and its fiefdoms and enlarged the territory of Muscovy. Married to the niece of the last Emperor of Byzantium, Ivan III appropriated the symbols of Byzantine power by bestowing upon himself the title of caesar (emperor), which is "tsar" in Russian, and by using the double-headed eagle of Byzantium in his coat of arms. The first Russian Metropolitan anointed him "Tsar of all Russia crowned by God". By the time Ivan III died, in 1505, Russia had become a state.

This holy alliance between church and state was strengthened in 1589 when the office of the Metropolitan of Moscow became the Patriarchate of All Russia. The alliance was soon rife with conflict, but it established absolutism based on divine right under Ivan IV, know as "Ivan the Terrible", who reigned from 1530 to 1584.

Dogmatically and intellectually weak, the Orthodox Church soon had to rely on the tsar's benevolence for its authority. This led to a decline of Christianity, beginning in the seventeenth century. During this time the rural population began to move away from the official religion and devote itself to local or regional variants. The Archimandrite Nikon tried to introduce reforms that would simplify the rites and reduce the pomp without changing basic dogma, uninspiring as it was. He also tried to improve the moral fiber of the clergy, many of whom were married or alcoholic. He even got the tsar to ban the sale of vodka on Sundays and religious holidays.

Nikon's mistake, however, was interfering with the magical and almost pagan nature of certain rites and practices of these simple believers. For such seemingly trivial matters as how one makes the sign of the cross, some of the faithful rebelled under the leadership of Avvakum. It was Avvakum, son of a pope from the Volga region, who created the sect of the Old Believers. In the period 1680 to 1690, twenty-five thousand of his followers set themselves on fire in acts of self-immolation to experience the delights of martyrdom and the joys of paradise. Many of them inflicted intense pain upon themselves, living lives of severe austerity. Avakum was finally exiled to Siberia and died at the stake in 1682. This period was the crucible of nationalism and xenophobia, a time when conversion to Orthodoxy signified becoming

Russian. All foreigners, even ambassadors to Moscow, were suspect and came under close surveillance.

Russia at this time had already begun its historical lag behind Western Europe. But the Russians remained wary of any change. Without an intelligent, civilizing Church to lead it, the enlarged Muscovite State, more than ever, needed a great tsar.

It was Peter the Great (1682-1725) who led Muscovy out of its backwardness and established the first real links with the people and ideas of Western Europe. Proclaimed tsar at the age of ten on Red Square, he soon reformed Russia thanks to the knowledge he acquired during his travels abroad. He was the first tsar to visit the "infidels", those "non-Christians", Catholic or Protestant, in the West... He also conceived of a Greater Russia before abolishing the patriarchate of Moscow in 1721 and replacing it with the Holy Synod, the new ecclesiastical authority which included an imperial high commissioner.

The higher clergy acquiesced to the tsar's changes, but the priests and some of the faithful rebelled, joining in the condemnations voiced by the Old Believers who saw the Antichrist in this reforming tsar. They were persecuted, like all conservatives. Peter the Great reduced the number of monks, who he forced to work, and imposed a tax on men who wore beards. The persecution resulted in an anti-Russian, anti-Slavic tendancy that carries on to this day. The reign of Catherine II, at the end of the eighteenth century, did not improve relations between Church and State. Indifferent to the anticlericalism directed against the popes, "those bearded ignoramuses", the sovereign confiscated land from the Church. During the same period, the high commissioner overseeing the Holy Synod declared he was an atheist.

The relationship between the Church and the State began to change, at least in spirit, with Alexander I, the mystical tsar who reigned until 1825. Nicolas I, who succeeded him, laid even greater emphasis on religious life, thereby provoking the controversy between liberal westernizers and Orthodox Slavophiles, attached to the past. Under the more open reign of Alexander II, who was assassinated on the day a somewhat liberalized constitution was proclaimed, the nihilists unconsciously linked up with Russia's mystical

RELIGION

tradition. Alexander III, a man indifferent to his era and to progress, was a "divine and Orthodox" tsar. Nicolas II, the last of the Romanovs, brought religion and empire into disrepute by accepting the presence of the scandalous "monk", Rasputin, the confidant of the Empress who contributed to the dynasty's collapse.

It is a strange paradox that it was an Orthodox priest who led the revolting masses toward the Winter Palace in St. Petersburg (now Leningrad) on January 9, 1905. However, the icons carried by the crowd did not stop the soldiers' bullets on this "red Sunday", which was a dress rehearsal for the Revolution of 1917.

Today, almost three centuries after Peter the Great brought the Church under his heel, the official who heads the Council of Religious Affairs in the USSR is still an atheist. However, a patriarch presides over the internal affairs of the Russian Orthodox Church and, in 1988, because of the more benevolent atmosphere under Gorbachev, he was allowed to resettle in Moscow. That same year, the Russian Orthodox Church celebrated its millenium with much pomp, a far cry from Stalin's brutal persecution and Khrushchev's more subtle oppression. Long gone are the days when Yaroslavsky, chairman of the Union of the Godless, had his "five-year plan for atheism" adopted by decree. This plan of the early 1930s was yet another whose objectives were not achieved, since it called for the elimination of every place of worship in the USSR by May 1, 1937.

Today there are about 7,000 Orthodox churches in use throughout the country, and all religions are benefitting from Gorbachev's reforms, even such a marginal sect as the Hari Krishna. But above all, Gorbachevism has turned the country's Christians into ordinary citizens, even though atheism remains the official credo. Practiced mostly by women, the Orthodox religion is beginning to find favor among the young without effecting any significant change in its conservative, even obscurantist, traditions. The triumphant Church that displayed the splendors of its millennial celebrations to thousands of guests is the eternal Russian Church, with its rites, its myths, and its anachronisms. It is the indestructible ally of the slavophile tendancy — xenophobic and anti-Semitic — making its ugly comeback. Surprisingly, it is also the pragmatic ally of Communist Party conservatives.

RELIGION

THE SECT OF THE OLD BELIEVERS IN MOSCOW

The Old Believers occupy a number of churches in Moscow and practice several rival rites, some even without priests. They are particularly numerous in Siberia, where they fled from the persecution of several intolerant tsars. Women must cover their heads with a white scarf for important ceremonies and virtually all the men wear beards.

WOMEN AS THE GUARDIANS OF DOGMA

After centuries of persecution the ban against Orthodoxy was lifted in 1988 on the occasion of the religion's millennial celebrations. The Old Believers, still militant conservatives, remain committed to their beliefs. These old women and the few remaining men look like figures from the 17th century lost in the 20th century. They are wary of visitors, who must virtually sneak in for a glimpse of the 18th century Cathedral of the Intercession of the Virgin, adjacent to the sect's amazing and immense cemetery in Moscow.

RELIGION

RELIGION

RELIGION

ORTHODOX CELEBRATION OF ST. NICHOLAS

The Orthodox rite is very ceremonious, but the ceremonies all seem similar because of their length, their pomp, and their superb chants. This religion, painstakingly codified, has retained complex rituals. The celebration of St. Nicholas on December 19th requires the presence of a Metropolitan (the head bishop in a province). In this church of Volokolamsk, some 60 miles from Moscow, the ceremony lasts almost three hours. The faithful remain standing because Orthodox places of worship have no seats.

A PRIEST AND A LABORER AT ST. DANIEL'S MONASTERY

After serving under Stalin as a "reception center" for the children of prisoners and of political deportees, then as an umbrella factory, this monastery complex in Moscow was returned to the Church on the occasion of the millennium in 1988. Church authorities spent 50 million roubles of their own funds to completely restore the complex. The Patriarch now resides here.

RELIGION

RESTORED CHURCHES

The renovation of the churches of St. Daniel's monastery was completed a few days before the millennial celebrations. Some religious paintings were brought here from museums, but most of the art work was completely restored. The project took lay and religious artists less than three years to complete, after learning the necessary techniques from former icon painters.

CATHOLIC MASS ON PALM-SUNDAY IN MOSCOW

Although they make up the majority of the population in Lithuania, there are not many Catholics in the capital. Their parish, headed by a very old priest, is often looked down upon by Westerners in Moscow. These visitors prefer to attend services led by an American priest whose presence is insured under an old agreement between the USA and the Soviet Union.
In Moscow, as elsewhere, Orthodox and Catholics ignore each other.

RELIGION

RELIGION

ANNUAL PILGRIMAGE IN SYSKOZHE

In the Ulyanovsk region, some 600 miles east of Moscow, a remarkable cohort of the old faithful, essentially women, sets out on the annual journey to the village of Syskozhe. Their pilgrimage, starting around May 22nd, is to honor St. Nicholas, whose face is said to have appeared in a miraculous spring.
Not even the harassment of the local authorities can stop this highly ritualized cult from their sacred undertaking.

A RELIGION OF NATURE

Behind the rituals venerating an Orthodox saint these old women in the fields and *taiga* (forests) instinctively revert to pagan rites dating back to the Russ (Russian) of the 10th century, before their conversion.
The Greek priests fiercely fought against these practices which made nature, earth, water, wind, and the huge forest into divinities worshipped by all Slav tribes.

RELIGION

RELIGION

OFFERINGS TO ST. NICHOLAS

Near the miraculous spring worshippers organize a service of offerings to the venerated saint and to nature. Offerings are blessed before being consumed at the end of this pilgrimage. This rite has long survived without the intervention of priests, but always under the watchful eye of the local political authorities.

RELIGION

IMMUTABLE RITES

It is the women who transmit, orally and in writing, the details of complex rites and the "signs" that continue unchanged from one century to the next.

RELIGION

NEAR THE MIRACULOUS SPRING

With candles and food these women recreate a church in the open air. This is a practice similar to that of the Old Believers who fled to Siberia to escape the persecution of Peter the Great.
On their trip home, these women will sprinkle the miraculous water around them as they go.

HOLY WATER

Essential ingredients in the communion with nature, the water and immersion rites symbolize the original baptism.
They are performed each year to secure one's place in paradise. A growing number of miraculous springs are discovered by religious women who often form sects around them. Today they are even found in the parks of Moscow.

RELIGION

RELIGION

RELIGION

IN THE SYNAGOGUE

There are two synagogues in Moscow. That's enough for a religion that is so little practiced; but, like other religions in the USSR, Judaism is experiencing a revival. Soviet Jews are not as interested in gaining more freedom to worship as they are in acquiring the right to emigrate to Israel and to learn and teach Hebrew. Considered a nationality, in the same vein as some one hundred other Soviet nationalities, Soviet Jews were designated their own territory, Birobidzhan in Soviet Asia, and an official language, Yiddish, the traditional language of Eastern European Jewry.

JEWS AT PRAYER

In the past few years all the Jewish refuseniks, imprisoned because they openly expressed the wish to leave the country, have been freed. For the several thousand who emigrated (9,000 in 1987), Israel has often been only a stepping-stone to the United States. The change in the official attitude does not solve the problem of a latent, "traditional" anti-Semitism. This is particularly evident in the writings and speeches of the Slavophile association Pamyat, which means "memory."

RELIGION

MUSLIMS IN MOSCOW

The only mosque in the capital was almost destroyed to make way for the construction of an Olympic stadium which was eventually built next to it. The mosque is attended by Sunni Muslims, particularly by descendants of the Volga Tatars. However, religious practice is not highly developed among the Muslims, many of whom do not live in their own regions or home republics.

RELIGION

AN EXPANDING RELIGION

The Soviet Union is currently experiencing an Islamic revival, part of the general trend toward Muslim fundamentalism. The traditions and customs, including forced marriages and the practice of dowries, have never really disappeared from the Muslim republics.
As in Orthodoxy, this revival is manifested by the construction of new mosques. The authorities, however, are distrustful of Koranic writings coming from abroad.

RELIGION

THE BAPTISTS OF LENINGRAD

Faithful Protestants, divided like the other cults by political or theological schisms, practice a religion whose stringency and austerity contrast sharply with the customary gold and glitter. In addition to the Adventists, the Pentacostalists, and the Lutherans of the Baltic, the Baptist Church represents a quiet force of over 500,000 followers whose center of activity lies in the Ukraine.

AMERICAN-STYLE PRACTICES AND PLACES OF WORSHIP

Constantly gaining more followers among the population, the Baptists also stand out by the way they welcome people of different faiths. The places of Protestant worship are oddly reminiscent of those of the American Far West, even though they have existed in Russia since the end of the 18th century.

RELIGION

FLAG BEARER

Soviet parades, whether civilian, as on May 1st, or essentially military, as on the anniversary of the Revolution in November, are always organized in minute detail. In every business establishment or organization there are volunteers responsible for the distribution of flags, balloons, paper flowers, and other bits and pieces. This does not prevent the participants from taking these things less and less seriously.

THE PARTY

Living under a single party system has been unbearable, but extremely difficult to change. In the past, the Soviets tried to circumvent the problem. Tens of thousands of informal associations now provide fierce competition for the Party throughout the country, a direct result of Gorbachev's new openness. Since 1987 they have called into question all the Communist organizations and bodies that used to pull all the strings and control people's every move.

For example, who could still take seriously the Soviet Society for the Protection of Nature, with its 28-30 million members who pay dues of a couple of kopecks each? Other spontaneous groupings have taken over from these languishing official bodies, part of the jammed "transmission belt" of the multiform Party whose power is intertwined with that of the State.

The Party is an obsession, a career, a target of derision and jokes, a dream, a refuge, a father, a mother, a religion, a goal, a routine, a state within the State, a habit, a nightmare, a social service, an insurance company, rites and rituals, parades and processions, leaders, many many leaders, a source of pleasure, touching sincerity, a comedy, a farce. The Party has a finger in every pot, dishing out apartments, cars or dachas, busying itself with everything imaginable. For a long time it was also a source of fear, a kind of Big Brother, comprised of an estimated 16-18 million members watching over everyone. But things are slowly changing...

Memories of some of the Party's past glories are fading because the Revolution is already seventy years old and, although the young are keeping alive the memory of the twenty million who perished fighting fascism during the Second World War, the number of those who lived through the War is dwindling. Added to those memories are the millions who fell victim to Stalin. They are even more deeply engraved in people's minds, as seen in the current literature and even in petitions. Since early 1988, by popular demand, monuments have been erected in several republics in memory of those who perished under the cruel dictator.

Yet, exact calculation of how many were massacred under Stalin has signficance only to historians. And it makes no sense today to reproach the Soviets or the Party for these atrocities since the master murderer and all his accomplices have been denounced, and the tyrannical movement named after him, Stalinism, repudiated. Even his museum, in his native town of Gori, in Georgia, has been closed "for repairs". The "Little Father" of the people, as he was called, is now making the headlines under more sinister epithets, accused of a wide range of evils by those who miraculously escaped him. An army of ghosts is sweeping across the country as the Soviet Communist Party exhumes its dead and unearths the tragic mistakes that blackened its history. It is striving to rise again from all those ashes. The Party has erred, the Party continues.

The Party still rules, but no longer reigns alone. The Party bosses are still around, defending their privileges and their concept of Socialism. Under Stalin and Brezhnev they felt secure, but now under Gorbachev these hundreds of thousands of Party bosses, without much conviction, have been seasoning their hackneyed speeches with *perestroika* and *glasnost*. The sad thing is that they have failed to understand that Gorbachev is not just a passing fad, a way of clearing the air. They ask themselves the old question: "what do we do now?" And the answer is obvious: "resist..." The middle ranks of the Party often choose to dig themselves in, holding on to their positions for the sake of Socialism and in the name of Lenin, invoked everywhere. Soviet television has at last revealed that Lenin had secretly warned the Party to watch out for Stalin. Also on TV, iconoclasts reflect on the meaning of the word "democracy"...

Gorbachev and his team have been eager to give meaning to words that had become empty shells. From the schools up to the highest levels of the State, the Party told stories no one listened to any more. The important thing was to pretend. In factories, offices, department stores, in the Party cells of the neighborhood... everywhere, the Party had become inert, basking in its privileges great and small. The privileged few in the Party were and are still known as the *Nomenklatura*. They celebrated May 1st as a sunny, family outing and the snow-filled parades of November 7th as a solemn anniversary which threatened the health of the grim, soft-hatted mummies who sat in front of Lenin's mausoleum and lorded over the festivities. The ceremonies are still there, and so is the headgear, but the faces underneath are new. After considerable initial hesitation, they are now calling this a new revolution, a revolution that has rehabilitated the Princess Bukharin, and a few other names long buried in oblivion. There are even those who are starting to whisper a name that has been both disgraced and forgotten, Trotsky. Who knows if, one day... ?

The Party, lulled to sleep, mummified, wilted, worn and faded, is responding badly to the electro-shocks intended to give it back a soul, an identity. It's difficult to treat schizophrenia with classic remedies, for the patient puts up a struggle, showing the world the contradictory faces of his split personality. Dr. Jekyll and Mr. Hyde inhabit the Politburo with the same certainties of the past. These certainties are garbed in the same ideology and the same words. Everywhere the uncomradely comrades are doomed to perpetual confrontation. Worn down by the perennial conflict between conservatives and modernists, the single Party should split itself in two, but it can't — by definition, by nature, and because of its total inertia.

The more they clash and contradict each other's efforts, the more the State and the Party are growing farther apart. At the same time a civil society is emerging. Big cities and republics where the Party has become a kind of mafia are being jolted and shaken up. Elsewhere, the reformist waves from Moscow cause but a mere ripple. The Communist Party of the Soviet Union continues to carry on in the far-flung provinces and rural areas as if the winds of history never blew. Indeed, there are areas where there has been no wind for a very long time...

The Party has decided, in the person of its General Secretary, that it should be somewhat restored to its proper place in society. But who knows what place that is?

THE PARTY

HISTORICAL COMMEMORATIONS

The further one gets away from Moscow and the big cities, the more the official events turn out to be cheerful occasions. For example, the 70th anniversary celebration of the October Revolution held in Astrakhan in November 1987 was a particularly relaxed affair. Forgetting ideology, the participants just threw a big party for all to enjoy.

MEMORIES OF THE WAR

The anniversary of the victory of 1945 is celebrated joyously on May 9th, though there is also a note of gravity. Sporting all their medals, the Soviets commemorate the millions who died and the destruction their country suffered.
No family was entirely spared by this war. Since vodka started flowing less liberally, these commemorations in Moscow's Gorky Park and elsewhere have lost some of their good humor. However, what they've lost in good humor, they've gained in good behavior.

36

THE PARTY

THE PARTY

ANNIVERSARY OF THE REVOLUTION IN ASTRAKHAN.
All official ceremonies in this region are held in the shadow of the Astrakhan cathedral, and the celebration of the 70th anniversary of the October Revolution was no exception.
Astrakhan, in the splendid delta of the Volga River, is one of those Soviet cities belonging to both Asia and Europe.

AND IN MOSCOW
At every ceremony soldiers are more or less on duty. They are ubiquitous at the celebrations of the October Revolution held in early November, but virtually absent from the May 1st parades. Like soldiers everywhere they must stand guard for hours on end, no doubt a far cry from the exaltation seen on the official propaganda posters on Red Square.

THE PARTY

THE PARTY

AFTER THE CONCERT

No parade is complete without music. Here, in front of the Bolshoi theater in Moscow, police musicians have finished playing in their band and are piling up their chairs and putting away their instruments. Today, each one has his own task, assigned by organizers who spend weeks preparing for the event. In a few minutes municipal cleaners will find all the obstacles removed, just in time for their scheduled job.

THE PARTY

MAY 1ST ON RED SQUARE

Behind the thin military cordon that keeps marching to and fro in a designated area, the population lines up in a most disorderly fashion, having waited hours for the pleasure, honor or duty to enter the Square. That day, except for a brass band, there was not a single soldier filing past the soft-hatted members of the Politburo dominating Red Square in front of the Lenin Mausoleum. Already an image of the past, it will live on in people's memories for a long time to come.

THE PARTY

LABOR DAY IN THE STREET

On May 1st in Moscow and elsewhere all the local bands turn out to take part in the parade and in the small get-togethers preceding it. The grand plan of the day brings out bits of the parade from all corners of the city.

WOMEN SWEEPERS

For centuries women have been sweeping the streets of Russia for a mere pittance. Their equipment is ancient but there are so many sweepers that the streets of Moscow and most other Soviet cities are always impeccably clean, though the road surface is sometimes rather bumpy. The cities also benefit from one of the largest armies of street-cleaning cars in the world.

THE PARTY

GOING HOME AFTER THE SHOW

The 70th anniversary of the Revolution was not celebrated with impeccable discipline everywhere. In Astrakhan, far away from Moscow, troops do not always withdraw in perfect order. Here there are no foreign correspondents or ambassadors to impress, and revolutionary fervor is no longer what it used to be.

THE PARTY

THE PARTY

TRIBUTE TO THE LIBERATORS

In Volokolamsk, in the Moscow region, a delegation of priests turns out each year to lay flowers at the foot of the monumental statues commemorating the liberation of the city in 1941. The date of this anniversary, December 19th, coincides with that of the feast of St. Nicholas, patron saint of the city. Even though these massive symbols of the Soviet past appear somewhat outdated, the USSR, including the Church, is still united in the commemoration of a war for which it suffered more than any other country in Europe.

EMBLEMS IN THE WINDOW

Symbols and pious images of the Party are less and less evident in daily Soviet life. Since the rise of Gorbachev, slogans, portraits, banners and Communist knick-knacks are becoming more discrete after invading Soviet life for years. It's as if the symbols are finally catching up with the reality; ideology has faded into the background.

PICTURES SOLD IN THE STREET

In the streets of Leningrad, Moscow, and Kiev painters and illustrators gather, trying to tempt passersby into buying their works. The profusion of all kinds and qualities of pictures has somewhat dampened the city strollers' passion for street art, but they still show up to look.

ART AND CULTURE

The day Mikhail Gorbachev allowed Andrei Sakharov to return to Moscow from exile in Gorky, the Soviet leader won the respect of the intellectuals who had been watching him with interest for some time. Freeing the regime's most hated and respected dissident was as remarkable and significant as the standing ovation the academicians gave Sahkarov, a fellow member of the Academy of Sciences. He had, in fact, never been stripped of his academician's title. In liberating Sakharov, Gorbachev was taking a calculated risk of unleashing the forces of creativity that had been fettered for decades. Sakharov's return represented a promise for some and an outrage for many others, who, because of a sense of duty or blind conviction, had dragged him through the mud.

From the ambiguous Stalin, who needed to have a court of admirers, to the uncultivated Brezhnev, who unabashedly accepted the Lenin prize for literature, the leaders of the Soviet Union always dreaded the intellectuals. Depending on the propaganda and foreign image needs of the moment, as well as who was in a stronger position, those in power would slacken or tighten the leash that held the intellectuals in place. Soviet realism, the officially sanctioned means of artistic expression, was the best remedy for restraining the intellectuals' flights of fancy. It was also the most prudent way to limit art to depicting positive images, for example those Communist heroes who broke production or cow-milking records. But all things must come to an end.

The non-figurative and religious painters regularly dispersed by the police only a few years ago can now, thanks to *glasnost*, exhibit their work in Moscow's Izmaylovo Park. The police don't even bother to look at what they are showing passers-by, masterpieces or the dregs. The people themselves are getting somewhat blasé after seeing so many nudes, triumphant Christs, and tedious copies of Cubism.

Even the avant-garde has its avant-garde. Many of the paths of Ismaylovo Park are being deserted by artists who refuse to rub shoulders with "Sunday painters" or the "protégés of the authorities" and, therefore, find other places to show their work. Just being persecuted by the authorities is no longer all it takes to be considered an artistic genius. In July 1988, the English auction house, Sotheby's, organized the world's first auction of modern Soviet painting, and the USSR's star painters as well as their most obscure ones learned first hand about the fragility and elusiveness of the fame they dreamed of achieving in the West.

The boldness of the painters is matched by the iconoclasm of the theater, cinema, and literature. They decry conservatism and Stalinism. Everyone is well informed by the few newspapers and magazines, which, against all the odds, have been supporting the revival of the intelligentsia desired by the General Secretary. Gorbachev, considered the first intellectual leader since Lenin, believes that the transformation of his country also depends on intelligence and that intellectuals have a role to play in educating the young and the population at large. Freedom of expression is their reward.

Obviously, this position does not enthrall the intellectuals of the bureaucracy who have been managing the arts as the petty guardians of ideology. No wonder they regard the publication of *Doctor Zhivago* and the rehabilitation of its author, Boris Pasternak, as an insult to good taste and Socialism. They feel the same way about the publication of the astounding and accusatory *Children of the Arbat* by Anatoly Rybakov and the transformation of protest singer-poet Vladimir Vissotsky into a national hero. And the same goes for those actors who prance about the stage half naked or the Georgian film producer Tenguiz Abuladze, who finally achieved fame in the Soviet Union for denouncing Stalin and all dictatorships in his film *Repent*. The output of literary works in recent years has been abundant, producing such diverse books as *The Wolf's Dream* by Tshinguiz Aytmatov and a scandalous, astonishing book written by an outspoken Leningrad call girl.

Publishers can hardly keep up with the avalanche of texts sent to them after laying dormant in people's drawers for years. They had been blacklisted by the official censors that the artists' and writers' unions are now trying to neutralize. But the institution of censorship is somewhat successfully resisting change since it has its share of supporters within the Party apparatus. While the censor may disappear, the bureaucrat remains. Although his role is threatened, he can always find a good excuse to keep on harassing artists. Blaming everything on the problems of central planning, the frightened and angry bureaucrat can delay delivery of paper supplies, and thus slow down a rise in circulation for those publications dedicated to the struggle for freedom and democracy.

War has been openly declared between conservatives and modernists. It's a battle without mercy where all is permitted, and the Soviet press has been having a field day with the division and permanent polemic. This is obviously disheartening to the guardians of Socialist order, who thought nothing would change on the road to Communist paradise. Now people are even saying, with the blessings of some in power, that maybe there is no such paradise, or, at the least, that it should be re-envisaged, and that the long-glorified past was an abomination. These past horrors are described in detail in books and articles of those who want to bear witness to a population which suspected what was going on, but had no idea about the magnitude of the disaster. Sometimes people refuse to believe it. On live TV programs new talent and new stars are sometimes discovered when people denounce Stalinist crimes.

But the most important recent development has been the emergence or reappearance of great writers who vividly portray all the lives lost in oblivion and terror. They are increasingly impatient with the unbearable sluggishness of the Party machinery, which, in turn, is defending itself against these writers who no longer respect all the Party holds sacred.

Since 1986 every day has been a treat for television viewers and the many readers of books and newspapers. They continue to ask for more of this critical and controversial literature, indifferent to the clamors of Party conservatives and the Slavophile extreme right.

ART AND CULTURE

ART AND CULTURE

THE PAINTER ALEXEI SUNDUKOV

In addition to the aesthetic boldness often seen in Western art, a great deal of Soviet art includes political criticism. It provokes and derides official images, or it transforms religious art — all of which got artists into trouble with the police in Brezhnev's day.

AN EXHIBITION AND A STUDIO IN MOSCOW

After spending years as semi-underground painters, artists such as Sergey Tshutov and Vladimir Naumyetz, shown here, are now exhibiting their work in a more open and competitive artistic climate. Many aspiring artists are taking their canvasses and compositions out of studios, long reserved for a select few. Now that everyone can show and sell his work without belonging to a "union", posterity will have to distinguish the painters of true genius from those who sometimes have only past persecution as a claim to fame.

ART AND CULTURE

IN IZMAYLOVSKY PARK IN MOSCOW

After setting up an unofficial market in the Bytsa Woods, artists and craftsmen were granted authorization to establish an official market in Moscow's Izmaylovsky Park. Since tens of thousands of Muscovites had flocked to the artistic meeting place in the woods, the authorities decided in 1987 to allocate a space in the park for the artists, which was larger and less precarious than the one in the woods.

RESTORATION OF ICONS

Despite the torments that have marked the existence of their schismatic community since the 17th century, the Old Believers have preserved treasures of artistic tradition.
Found among them are the best icon restorers, whose workshop near their patriarchate in Moscow is always bustling with activity. The artists there are more hospitable to visitors than the stern *babushkas* (grandmothers) in the churches.

VADIM ZAKHAROV IN HIS STUDIO

Vadim Zakharov is one of the talented artists whose star is rising in Moscow. Astute Soviet art lovers are buying paintings, speculating on a rapid rise in value. Westerners also buy the canvasses of these *glasnost* painters, either directly or in the public sales held in one of Moscow's centrally located churches. Some Soviets have publicly criticized the government for allowing the export of the country's works of art in order to acquire foreign currency.

ART AND CULTURE

ART AND CULTURE

ART AND CULTURE

QUICK PORTRAIT

Portrait painters have invaded a part of Nevsky Avenue in Leningrad, the Arbat pedestrian street in Moscow, and many other public places. In spring and summer, sometimes even in winter wearing mittens, these artists entice provincial passersby for a sitting. Their art brings them a comfortable income (10-15 roubles per portrait). Not bad, even if the competition is getting ever tougher.

POPULAR ART

Neither sleet nor snow can keep away lovers of street art, although that kind of weather isn't exactly conducive to creating work of great genius.
These "painters", with their mass-produced canvasses, liven up certain drab neighborhoods.
Avant-garde art certainly hasn't taken to the streets, the favorite haunt of decorative painters who evoke flowery images of spring in the dead of winter.

ART AND CULTURE

LEONID TALOTSHKYN, ART COLLECTOR

Held in contempt, dreaded, hounded, ripped up, hidden, and denounced, the nude has only recently made a timid but notable appearance in painting. But "pornography" remains the bugbear of a prudish regime, a taboo for both the Orthodox Church and the Party.
Even though legislation is becoming more lenient, most Soviets are not prepared to freely discuss "those things" or accept topless sunbathers on the beaches.

ART AND CULTURE

THE SINGER TATYANA IVANOVNA

In the twilight of their lives women and men are starting to bear witness to their years under Stalin. At the age of 86 Tatyana Ivanovna Sukhomlyna receives great acclaim at her concerts, singing of an existence which led her from an American husband to the Gulag via an eventful life in Paris. Born of noble stock, she has never renounced her religion nor her outspokenness. For this she paid dearly, seven years of internment and many long, dark years without recognition and appreciation. Finally recognized and celebrated, she has just made her first record.

FASHION

Early in 1988, when a pretty Soviet girl went to a cooperative market to buy her first T-shirt with Lenin and *perestroika* emblazoned on her chest, the old Communists knew their world was coming to an end. Leave it to fashion to destabilize an ideology reduced to rituals...

Vladimir Ilich would have perhaps smiled and "his" poet, Vladimir Mayakovsky would certainly have applauded this new living art form appearing in the streets under the impassive gaze of the last Stalinists of the 1970s. The dress of young Soviet women had already begun to brighten up the drab streets when Brezhnev's overbearing portrait still adorned the walls. It was just one sign among many that society was changing.

The *babushkas* in their multicolored head-scarves chattering in front of the old buildings of Moscow still can't understand how their daughters' daughters, brought up with respect for the Party, God, Lenin, and the neighbors, can walk around with a reproduction of the church on Red Square on their backs or between their breasts. They cross themselves exclaiming *"Bozhemoy!"* (my God), like they did a few years ago on seeing the first miniskirts.

Quite spontaneously, out of the irrepressible need to assert themselves, women in the early 1980s began to reject the drabness and uniformity of existing fashion, and to create what they couldn't find in the shops, or in Soviet realism. It was a fashion of liberation, born in the big cities, but quickly spreading to the provinces.

The sensible chic of German fashion as seen in the dog-eared copies of the West German fashion magazine, *Burda Moden*, wasn't enough for Soviet women any more. Since 1987 over 500,000 copies of the magazine have been printed in Russian four times a year, but the German-Soviet joint venture has neither met demand nor satisfied the new craving for elegance and originality. This glossy magazine is a showcase for the established fashion trends of the West, with advertisements for perfumes, creams, and cat food. It's a consumer's dream in a country where one is never sure of finding the bare necessities of life. It provokes a longing for the extraordinary in people not sure they should harbor such desires.

Even Slava Zaytsev, who became the USSR's leading designer after years of discreet accomplishment, seems the classicist in his elegant fashion house on the Avenue of Peace in Moscow compared with the avant-garde who insolently show off in fashion shows, shops, and on the street.

This is essentially a women's revolution. The men confine their audacity and fashion urges to jeans, gadgets, and embellishments for their cars. In the world of clothes, as in many other domains, women are way ahead of men. They're freer, more inventive, more mature and younger at the same time. But men match them in their desire to distinguish themselves from other members of their sex. Because it's still not for the masses, fashion helps people stand out from the masses. In this world once thought immobile, women are the first to express their individuality and shed the burden of conformity. Rejecting the past, fashion has proved to be a harbinger of *glasnost* and *perestroika*. It has also created a gap between young women and those of the older generation, the staunch vestals of Communism and Mother Russia.

Often fashion is the stuff that dreams and luxury are made of. Seamstresses and knitters working at home earn a good living by producing what planning officials for decades deemed futile. Women, however, consider fashion more and more indispensable and are even willing to put 200-300 roubles in the slightest piece of material made in Paris, London, or Rome.

Being beautiful is no longer a sin and women are no longer condemned, due to past wars and suffering, to dress as if they were in permanent mourning. Women are starting to win the right to futile pursuits and, indeed, they do indulge themselves in the saunas, Turkish baths, and massage parlors where urban society relaxes. So, fashion is in style. It's a remedy which parades the streets like a reproach to society. And it thumbs its nose at the stern Party leaders in their grim fedoras.

FASHION

A COUPLE IN THE STREET

Fashion has not yet reached the entire Soviet population, even in the big cities. Far from it, in fact. To distinguish yourself by your taste in clothes is still a kind of sin to some people. It's also sometimes financially prohibitive. However, the main obstacle is conformism, and in this domain, as in many others, men are the most conservative and the most resistant to the slightest change.

PRESENTATION OF A COLLECTION BY SLAVA ZAYTSEV

Slava Zaytsev, Moscow's leading fashion designer for women who want to get noticed without being shocking, has abandoned relative obscurity to make a splash on the nascent Soviet fashion scene. Each of his fashion shows is a sophisticated event. For a couple of kopecks passersby can enter the Fashion House on the Avenue of Peace and see his designs close-up. And if they wish, they can also place an order; the prices of dresses and summer and spring coats range from 90 to 400 roubles each.

FASHION

FASHION

FASHION

FASHIONABLE STYLIST AND COUPLE

In order to become known in an effervescent world generating numerous creative artists, designers must make sure they get noticed. The flashier their fashions, the more popular they are with the younger generation who try to adapt and improve on the bold tastes arriving from the West. Sometimes the young push their sense of fashion, even in street clothes, to the brink of the Soviets' sense of decency. The new laws governing independent work and cooperatives allow craft workshops to make and sell clothes in shops and markets provided they pay income taxes, which, of course, is not very popular.

AN EVENING OUT IN MOSCOW

Trendy and impatient young people, eager to keep up with the pace of a sometimes imaginary West, get together in apartments for lively parties and long vodka-drinking evenings. Russian traditions have enough power to leave their mark on the new imported trends and fashions.

FASHION

FASHION MODELS AT A LENINGRAD MARKET

Fashions are now liberating and provocative, a change as great as the reaction of these stallkeepers at the Leningrad market. Only a few years ago the women selling their wares in the market would have thrown tomatoes at these avant-garde models and chased them away. The designer of these new dresses deliberately arranged this exceptional encounter, a unique confrontation between two worlds which are light-years apart.

FASHION

THE YOUNG

For Party officials "young" means *Komsomol*, the Communist Youth League dedicated to the principles of democratic centralism. At its head, old youngsters keep organizing the same conventional leisure activities that no longer appeal to today's youth. It's an inescapable organization which young people attend to perform certain ritualistic duties, but they go elsewhere to seek their real pleasures and distractions. Indeed, the *Komsomols* had to rejuvenate their ideas and many of their leaders well before Gorbachev arrived on the scene.

The Party and the country have been blind to the fact that their youngsters have grown up. Like young people everywhere, Soviet youth rejects the outdated ideas of the older generation, upsetting their ideological metabolism. It's a never-ending story, an illness for which there is no cure, not even a Socialist one. For those who believed, or pretended to believe, that their youngsters had been effectively immunized against change, the surprise has been all the greater. The young punks, drifters, hippies, and rockers leave school and turn their backs on the *Komsomols*, where Lenin's gospel was once preached and Brezhnev's prose glorified to an increasingly indifferent congregation. The old Party crocodiles have given birth to a bunch of ducklings — and noisy ones at that. The rockers of the late 1970s, though their lyrics were still innocent, were already singing the death chant of an aging and deaf regime.

Gorbachev was still a Brezhnevite when the rock groups electrified fans in Leningrad and other places. In Leningrad, the Soviet capital of hip music and departure point for summer drifters, the municipal authorities, trade unions, and *Komsomols* had to set up a Rock Club for amateur groups back in 1983.

It was an attempt to recover lost ground, but it was also a sign that the aging Party bosses were beginning to realize that something was going on with their youth, that the spirit of the times had eluded the Plan, and that excommunication was no longer effective in exorcizing Western demons. Despite the *ukazes* (official decrees), boycotts, and bans, the records of the most inoffensive rock groups sold like hot cakes. By 1984 there were several thousand amateur rock groups in over a dozen Soviet republics. For the first time in decades official disgrace and condemnation fell on deaf ears, and a whole group in society quietly seceded even before its rock culture had become fashionable. It became urgent to recapture these defiant youngsters, so the Slavophiles and guardians of the Party rallied with xenophobic fervor around this endeavor. The battle was fierce. And it was also lost.

During the heroic days of the Leningrad Rock Club the undisputed king was Boris Grebenchikov, of the Aquarium rock group. At the time he was considered just an amateur singer, relegated to semi-clandestine appearances, even though he drew wildly enthusiastic crowds of young and not so young fans. He was untouchable, worshipped and denounced all at the same time. Since 1987, however, he is seen regularly on Soviet television, his hippy-style, irreverant appearance de rigueur. Starting in the early 1980s, under growing pressure from the young, the *Komsomols* — wary of seeing their flock stand up to cheer other bands — started organizing their own festivals. The police, after years of trying to get youthful audiences to sit and quiet down during concerts, finally gave up, both out of sheer exasperation and on orders from above. In certain faraway provinces, however, Communist authorities, referring to blacklists dating back to Brezhnev's time, persisted in banning these concerts. The lists were unofficial, their existence never openly acknowledged. They were drawn up by the Ministry of Culture during the days of the first hit parades, which were fixed by chief editors whenever the hot groups got too popular.

After years of apprehension about some of its young people, the USSR is now afraid of them. That's because the young broke the mold, and now it's impossible to make another one in the name of *perestroika* and *glasnost*. The molded ones have disappeared, replaced by young people who sometimes confront each other in two opposing camps, punks versus *Lubyeris*, for example. The former are Western-oriented dropouts, the latter shaven-headed nationalists who like body-building and karate, and are nicknamed after Lubyerts, the drab suburb of eastern Moscow where they first appeared.

As valiant scouts of Socialism, the Komsomols once organized a day of "dialogue" between these rival groups. Some participants pretended to talk to each other, unconscious of the snickering around them. It's clear that these "enemies" neither want nor intend to become reconciled. The USSR will have to live with its conflictual and irreconcilable youth. What do the rockers who hang out in Moscow and Leningrad have in common with the veterans of the Afghanistan war? Nothing. You can recognize these vets by their eyes, according to the film *Is It Easy To Be Young in the USSR?* This Soviet documentary created a scandal when it was released in Moscow in 1987, but was a sensation among the young. It described their existential angst and their confusion, and the indifference of adults. It was a unique first in a country where the young were, by definition, supposed to be happy, like everyone else. After all, they are the vanguard of Socialism...

Despite its whole system of thought, education, and drivel, in the end Communism has produced young people who are similar to young people everywhere. Some are good students who join the Pioneers and dream of joining the Party, some are good *Komsomols*, and some are parrots who repeat the sacred texts of Communism. Others don't even want to hear about politics. They're jeans hunters and John Lennon fans, or delinquents who rip things off from people's cars or apartments. They're the youth of the projects who hate where they live and get their kicks by vandalizing trains or buses. They're fans of Moscow's soccer team, Spartak, attacking other soccer fans. There are also guitar freaks who hit the road instead of going apple picking on the *kolkhozes*, shameless lovers who flaunt their affections before all, motorcycle fanatics who leave the police far behind in the chase, promiscuous young women who wear miniskirts and take the pill, beggars who sing or recite poetry for money in pedestrian streets, insolent students who sneer at their backwards teachers, iconoclasts who set up associations without seeking permission, idealistic environmentalists, dropouts on drugs, bad patriots who try to get out of military service, and many who are just bored — utterly bored.

The young girls, for example, are bored. They dream of one day shedding the uniform they must wear all year at school and college. They aren't allowed to indulge in the slightest personal whim. Even pants are forbidden, except for sports. The rules are symptomatic of a stagnant society that fails to keep up with its youth. Yet children are considered kings in the Soviet Union. In their dark brown skirts or pants and their red scarves or scarlet hair ribbons, from West to East, from Latvia to Kirgizia, they are present in all official festivities, symbolizing equality in the Soviet Union. They are well behaved and adulated in this world of shortages which has preserved the simple pleasures for them. Soviet children aren't consumers yet, and they still can marvel at the smallest treasure. One might think they feel browbeaten. In fact, they are totally naive and innocent. The difficulties arise later, but they're starting at an earlier and earlier age.

Soviet youth does not rebel. It dodges the issues, escapes, and then glides toward consumer society in a world that still has nothing superfluous to offer. But Pepsi, Coke, and millions of rock records don't provide a sufficient answer to their dilemma. Although drugs are no longer a taboo subject for the media, people in this puritan society still don't know how to talk about love, sex, or psychology. Impatiently, youth in the city does its own exploring, without guidance, while the youngsters in the provinces look on enviously.

Some young people are rediscovering religion. Wearing a necklace with a small crucifix around their necks is a symbol, an affirmation of their individuality. Above all, they're reinventing romanticism, with the big dream of distinguishing themselves in a world that holds them down. To a society that offered and still offers them life as part of a group, their response is often the desire to live in a gang.

THE YOUNG

FOUR LITTLE GIRLS

Throughout the Soviet Union children are cherished and even fawned on, almost as if they were an endangered species.
As in other industrialized countries the birth rate has dropped considerably over the past 15 years, even in the southern republics.
Still, the birth rate in the south remains higher than in the western part of the USSR.

THE BEGINNING OF THE SCHOOLYEAR IN SAKHALIN

On September 1st, some 6000 miles from Moscow, the ceremony marking the beginning of the school year proceeds in the same way it does throughout the rest of the country. Children wear uniforms in an attempt to erase all differences of race, culture, and social origin, not to mention class.

THE YOUNG

AN EXPERIMENTAL SCHOOL

The Soviet Union, too, carries out successful, but isolated, educational experiments. These schoolchildren in Pavlish, a little village in the Ukraine, benefit from an active pedagogy invented in the 1950s by Vassily Sukhomlnisky. It combines classical education with gardening, school management, and preparation of meals, including baking the bread these children eat every day.

THE YOUNG

THE YOUNG

CHILDREN AT PLAY IN KALININGRAD

Kids will be kids. In a country whose cities are not so clogged with cars, these children of Kaliningrad have turned their street into a veritable playground. Somehow there will always be an adult on hand to make sure they are not up to any mischief. Children in the USSR are at all times the collective responsibility of the population.

THE YOUNG

GYPSY CHILDREN IN ASTRAKHAN

In recent years the gypsies have regained some freedom to roam from place to place. This makes it difficult for their children to go to school since the authorities have not always designated a school district for them. The gypsies pursue their traditional occupations — basket weaving, horse breeding, even playing the violin.

THE YOUNG

SNOW CARNIVAL

The children of Moscow are the kings of the Snow Carnival, which takes place every year on the outskirts of the capital. Even in town children are born with skis on their feet. Cross-country skiing is very popular, particularly during the months of cold, clear weather when, after the snows of November, it is possible to ski in the street.

75

THE YOUNG

PUNKS IN LENINGRAD

Being a punk is a peculiarity confined to certain circles. It's sticking your tongue out at the Party or a provocative reference to the West, sometimes practiced jokingly by engineers or intellectuals pretending to be punks in the evening after a day of work. Times have changed and people no longer go to prison for dressing up as a punk.

DEVIATIONIST HAMMER AND SICKLE

Committing the supreme sacrilege, young people sometimes play around with the sacrosanct symbols of Socialism. Hammer and sickle are desecrated and Lenin himself has made a remarkable appearance on T-shirts, though his portrait has virtually disappeared from the streets. The apparatchiks who grew gray under Stalin and Brezhnev suffer in silence, blaming it all on Mikhail Gorbachev.

THE YOUNG

THE YOUNG

MUSICIANS OF THE ARBAT

Since the summer of 1987, musicians, guitarists, drifters, hippies, and dropouts have established their seasonal kingdom in the Arbat, Moscow's pedestrian street. They play their instruments, meet friends, and sometimes earn a couple of roubles. Despite some protests, their presence has now been accepted and the rare policeman in the area ignores them.

HIPPIES NEAR RIGA

These hippies have set up their summer camp in a pine forest near Riga. There they meet, sometimes after hitchhiking for thousands of miles. These road rats are now left in peace by the police, probably because they don't touch drugs. There are several thousands of them in Moscow and Leningrad alone.

SAILORS' PARADE

Navy Day in Leningrad in August 1988 did not attract crowds. However, for a small group of overexcited sailors it soon degenerated into a pretext for boozing and parading and blocking up traffic. In a matter of months such "demonstrations" have become a way of protesting and getting noticed. In Moscow the Veteran Parachutists Day, held during the same period, turned into a drinking bout in Gorky Park, with several participants injured, including policemen.

THE YOUNG

THE YOUNG

THE YOUNG

AT CARLOS SANTANA'S CONCERT

On the 4th of July in 1987, Carlos Santana gave a concert in Moscow to celebrate American Independence Day.
For many youngsters and adults America is an obsession, a model surpassing all others. From young rockers to economists, the only intelligible currency unit is often the worshipped dollar whose value is followed by the rouble — though non-convertible — both in banks and on the street.

CONCERT AND DEBATE ON DRUGS

In early 1987, at a big concert at the House of Physicians in Moscow, doctors and men of art officially discovered the evils of drugs. In a lively debate following the concert they clashed with young people who reproached them for never having discussed drugs before.
The doctors admitted that "before" this had been forbidden, even though drugs and especially certain pharmaceutical products have had a destructive effect on the young for years.
The subject is now regularly brought up by the press.

RUSSIAN VILLAGE

Pereslavl-Zalesky, 75 miles from Moscow, is a village identical to thousands of others that have remained virtually unchanged throughout the ages. It has the same dirt roads and wooden buildings as during the time of the tsars. The peasants are still poor, living outside a system they don't understand any more than the previous one. It's a system which has given up trying to understand them.

RURAL LIFE

Despite the brutal intensity with which agricultural collectivization was carried out, production records of the *kolkhoz* (collective farms) were broken only on paper and sparkling combine-harvesters were used primarily for propaganda, for example, in such films as Eisenstein's *The General Line*. These modern machines of the 1920s slowly rusted away under consecutive five-year plans while the village horses continued to work the fields at their slow but efficient pace. Miraculously, Stalin's bloody collectivization drive did not destroy all of Russia's traditional peasants. These *kulaks'* only wrongdoing was to have profited by the brief wave of liberalism permitted under the New Economic Policy. Introduced by Lenin in 1921, it was ferociously suppressed by Stalin starting in 1927. What a fascinating but cruel failure was this collectivization tornado, designed to create a completely new world! But the offensive that caused millions to die of hunger and despair neither transformed the peasantry nor the countryside. The peasants digested Socialism like they swallowed previous agricultural reforms, which merely reformed earlier plans. They patiently waited for revenge and rehabilitation. Perhaps such a time is now at hand.

The Promethean agriculture that fashions landscapes and feeds dreams of dominating nature still surrounds the peasantry of the *mir*, meaning both village and peace. These peasants watch city-style television in a decor reminiscent of the 1950s in Western Europe. While townspeople evolve, rustic *basbushkas* (grandmothers), unchanging and distrustful, sell their wares in cities they hardly understand. These cities may seem like hell to the peasants, but that's where the roubles are. Neither bullying, ridicule nor even disavowal and destruction have turned the peasants into revolutionaries or counter-revolutionaries. Eschewing reality, they have fenced themselves in staunch conservatism as though fossilized in the past. Thus, paradoxically, they perpetuate and contribute to the immobility of the regime. Still, they are worried about the world that is beginning to stir around them, turning the towns into veritable dens of iniquity.

Despite the *kolkhoz* complexes that have invaded the countryside, often turning little villages into rural slums, the wooden *isbas* (log huts), with their quaint, floral motif double windows, still dominate the Russian landscape all the way from Lake Baikal to the confines of Siberia, from one end of the USSR to the other. In contrast to the large, slope-roofed houses of the Baltic lands, the *isbas* go on and on throughout the country. They are all somehow alike, with their festooned entrances, green gates, woodpiles for winter, and closed verandas nestling to the side of the house where everyone drops their coats, boots, or heavy shoes. They look like picture postcards in pastel shades, the embodiment of Russian nostalgia. Fragile in the disproportionate vastness of the countryside, they seem to date back to a distant past. In fact, they are never more than a hundred years old. With television aerials perched on their roofs, the sole sign of modern times, these peasant palaces seem strange and ageless.

The turbulent years of Russian history have left the *isbas* unaffected, and so they survive, even on the outskirts of Moscow. There they look just like those in sleepy villages a thousand miles away. Stacked behind their windows are jars, bottles, fruit, flowers, and vividly colored objects that make people forget the cold and the ice crystals forming on the window panes. The cold hardens people to the elements, but the *isba's* primitive interior is always warm and cozy. The rare traveller is greeted with cordial hospitality in this hard, rough world. The *isba* is filled with the all-pervading fragrance of cabbage and wood, the ubiquitous smell of *samagon*, the home-distilled alcohol which peasants produce by the millions of gallons. This delicious bootleg drink is made from fruit or herbs, but can be dangerous when the less scrupulous home stills use wood shavings, yeast, or even tomato purée.

These mythical *isbas* of eternal Russia are houses from another world, where wolves still roam, and sleighs and troikas, now running at the Moscow race tracks, still ride.

RURAL LIFE

Often deserted or neglected, *isbas* today are being rediscovered by enraptured urbanites who are turning them into *dachas* (country homes). The peasants, now living in drab housing projects blessed with central heating and running water, miss their traditional dwellings. These *moujiks* (peasants) dream of the villages that certain planners deprived them of. And indeed, *isbas* are beginning to play a new role and regain political, social and economic favor. Farmers want to get back closer to the land after spending years as indifferent administrators, workers in an environment they no longer understand.

In recent years several novelists have recounted the story of this modern return to their peasant origins, this reawakened attachment to the land and nature. According to the ideologists, this attachment was a historical deviation that Communism had forever eradicated. But Valentin Rasputin, the Siberian writer, and others have marvelously reconciled the Russians with their land. Even before the arrival of Gorbachev, in an effort to renew Russia's naturalist tradition, they started to describe their beloved countryside, with its muddy and dusty villages blending in perfectly with the surrounding scenery.

The streets along which these houses stand, in more or less orderly rows, are rarely asphalted. While horse-drawn carriages are not rare, cars are virtually absent. More often than in town, personal transport is by motorcycle and heavily laden side-car, and by horse, plodding alongside huge tractors.

Village life is full of contrasts, difficult and harsh. Yet there is a strong sense of community, with the complex bonds of family and friendship forged in the past. Life often centers around a river and invariably around water supply points or village wells. Villages and collective facilities are reminiscent of life in the 1950s. Running water is rare, except in the larger buildings. This is in striking contrast with the grandiose ambitions of the agricultural plans, which can't even assure that a potato crop is harvested before the start of the rainy season. The productivity of crops grown on the *sovkhoz* or *kolkhoz* is ten times lower than that of small market gardens and private plots.

Private patches, individually cultivated, were rehabilitated some years ago and were very recently, and quite officially, praised for their important contribution to agriculture and the economy. Consequently, the authorities granted farmers the right to hold their plots under fifty-year renewable and transferable leases.

As the small patches grow larger, the myth of collectivization will die and the peasant will rediscover his traditional role in agriculture. Television and the press regularly report on the exploits of these successful agricultural "entrepreneurs", these small, private cooperatives relearning the secrets of successful, efficient farming techniques. Many of them make money and incur the envy of others. They have become a focus of criticism for jealous local politicians, who believe it sinful not to depend on a wage or salary for one's livelihood. With grave concern, they follow the activities of these farmers, who find relief in listening to Gorbachev's reformist speeches and reading newspapers which support their endeavors.

But deep down, the peasants remain worried. They still vividly remember the 1930s collectivization drive, when cows and other privately-owned animals were requisitioned by the authorities. It will take years to overcome this mistrust, accentuated by the reticence of local Party bullies, more at ease with the contrivances of the Plan than with the obstinate realities. These petty officials have a lot to learn from the Russian peasant. Veritable repositories of ancient wisdom, the farmers can sometimes unravel the mysteries of weather forecasting, a subject virtually ignored by agricultural planners.

In the vast Russian countryside the pace is set by these hybrid villages centered around *kolkhozes* and nineteenth century *isbas*. Seen from the train or the rare highway, the landscape of the *taiga* and the cleared plains goes on and on. Always the same, seemingly immobile, it's difficult to decide whether this landscape is monotonous or fascinating. The long journey across the Soviet Union by Trans-Siberian Railroad is like a loop film, dream and reality at the same time. The samovar is still heated with charcoal, its fragrances pervading the air every morning as the passengers awaken at daybreak. The territory of the Soviet Union is so vast that sunrise comes at widely different hours in various parts of the country...

Only by train can the traveller grasp the intensity and immensity of the Soviet countryside, an endless forest of conifers and birches, cut through by rivers and clearings. Curtains of trees go on for days, sweltering in the heat of the sun or buried in snow for months on end. The plains form an enormous expanse where all landmarks seem to have disappeared. They resemble the immobile landscapes of the Russian painter, Blaise Cendrars: no one knows whether he imagined this vastness or whether he actually travelled through it. Here nature is as rugged as the peasantry, whether from Siberia or from the luscious banks of the Volga, with a spring that bursts out, exploding into summer in a matter of weeks.

The strength, power, and above all, vastness of nature here is overwhelming. It's omnipresent, even up to the outskirts of Moscow. This is a country where many cities seem to have been built right in the countryside. Once you step past the last building, nature and the taiga stretch ahead, without a transition. It's a generous environment as well, a paradise of wild berries and mushrooms, and a fisherman's paradise, despite the mosquitoes proliferating in the swamps and marshes. They have not yet been drained by agriculture, that "evil genius" which has long watched over Russia and other parts of the land. It's a nature filled with birds, stopping for but a brief summer, and with buffaloes, slowly reappearing throughout the country thanks to a sanctuary south of Moscow.

This rural world seems likely to remain asleep for a long time unless its people simply decide to move away for good, indifferent to the reforms and speeches that continue to rain down on them like a natural calamity.

RURAL LIFE

RURAL LIFE

WATER DUTY

In most Soviet villages, near Moscow or thousands of miles away, running water is a mere dream and surfaced roads an unaffordable luxury. Despite these difficult living conditions, there is a growing movement to return to village living. After destroying thousands of villages to make way for *kolkhoz* building complexes, the regime now supports this resettlement trend.

DOING THE LAUNDRY IN THE RIVER

About 60 miles from Moscow laundry is still done in the river. The facilities in Russian country villages are similar to those in Western Europe during the 1930s. The pace of life is so different between town and country that there is a wide gap between villagers and city-dwellers. They live in completely different worlds.

RURAL LIFE

VILLAGE ACCORDIONIST

His work finished, a *kolkhoz* cow-milker wanders the streets playing the accordion.
The instrument is highly popular in the countryside and many television viewers miss the amateur accordion-playing contests that used to appear on Channel One.

POST OFFICE NEAR RIGA

All the grandeur of eternal Russia survives in this tranquil house, which stands on a dirt road in the village of Aspusiems, 60 miles from Riga. It is not a fairy tale post office, but is still open several hours a day, even receiving telegrams from abroad. It looks like it was invented by the local tourist office, but that doesn't even exist in this little Latvian village on the coast.

PEASANT WOMEN CULTIVATING A PRIVATE GARDEN

The cultivation of private plots of land plays an increasingly important role in Soviet food production, especially in Russia. It's not new, but its importance is now officially recognized and encouraged. It is mainly the women who till the soil; the men only take over for private market-gardening, which is also making rapid progress.

RURAL LIFE

RURAL LIFE

POTATO HARVEST IN A *KOLKHOZ* NEAR ULYANOVSK

Together with cucumbers, onions, and cabbages, potatoes are still the staple food in every household. Agricultural work in the Ulyanovsk area, in a cleared *taiga* where the soil is not always very rich, is very similar to such activities 600 miles away, near Moscow. The pace of work is not determined by the weather or the urgency of the task at hand. It merely depends on the good or bad habits of the farmers. The USSR has never succeeded in solving its agricultural problems, caused mainly by the peasants' lack of enthusiasm for collectivization. After the harvest the fruit and vegetables leave on a long and arduous journey during which millions of tons of potatoes are ruined, another waste due to faulty State planning.

RURAL LIFE

RURAL LIFE

RURAL LIFE

A PEASANT WOMAN AND HER SON

Interiors in the countryside all look alike, and life is very traditional. The peasants, and in general all rural Russians, maintain a kind of "Slavic lifestyle." They feel more and more removed from life in the towns and cities whose bustle and excesses they don't understand.

ENTRANCE TO THE FAMILY *ISBA*

Father and sons rest on the steps of their *isba* after a hard day's work near Ulyanovsk. Despite their very bare exterior, these Russian houses are very receptive inside. One always enters at the side of the house after taking off one's heavy winter gear. Most Russians in rural areas still know how to build or repair an *isba*.

RURAL LIFE

RURAL LIFE

INSIDE THE *ISBA*: THE MODERN CORNER...

Lenin has not taken the place of Christ or of the icon inside the rural dwelling. He has simply moved to another, more logical and modern, place on top of the television set. Television, still not as widespread as in the West, is becoming more pervasive throughout the USSR, even in regions where distractions are rare.

... AND THE TRADITIONAL CORNER

The *krasny ugol*, literally "the pretty corner," contains the icon, the cross, the pious images, and a candle which sometimes burns continuously. The construction of an *isba* must always start with this corner chapel. This tradition has not been lost and, even in the absence of religious practice, most families still devote one corner of their interior to the *krasny ugol*. Here the faithful recite their prayers every Saturday night and celebrate mass on Sundays.

FAMILY PORTRAIT

In the countryside, and to some extent in the towns, particularly in Russia, the feeling of belonging to a very large family remains very strong.

The continuing housing shortage, often obliging people to live together, is certainly as responsible for this sentiment as the solid traditions ensuring close bonds between young and old.

THE KREMLIN SEEN FROM THE MOSKVA RIVER

The quadrilateral shape of the Kremlin rising above the Moskva River is one of the most famous architectural complexes in the world. It was already renowned before the Revolution, and the square behind it was already "red" under the tsars. That's because the adjectives "red" and "beautiful" are the same word in Russian, *krasny*. Thus, the "Beautiful Square" has also been "Red" since the 17th century.

MOSCOW CAKE FACTORY

Impressive examples of industrial architecture from before and after the Revolution are located in the center and northeast of Moscow. All Muscovites know the smells of this cake factory occupying a large part of the island in the Moskva, not far from the Kremlin. The municipal authorities are planning to move the city's many large factories out of town, a change that would increase commuting time for many urban workers.

THE CITY

Crowds tend to differ from one city to another, but you find them everywhere, equally dense and overwhelming. Their vibrant energy, resembling the intensity of American crowds, perhaps explains the Soviets' burning desire for individuality. Crowds move easily down huge avenues that can accommodate scores of vehicles, even though these thoroughfares were designed at a time when the USSR had hardly a privately-owned automobile. Today, trucks, new and ancient, spit out their fumes carelessly, and the center of Moscow is increasingly paralysed by minor traffic jams, which the policemen prefer to ignore. Cars backed up, one behind the other, bother people less than the ultimate crime... changing lanes. Still, people have fallen madly in love with their cars, and they put a lot of their extra energy and money into finding the scarce, but necessary, spare parts for them. The fact is, cars cause more problems than they solve in the USSR, but everyone wants one. And that's something new. Year in, year out, the increasing auto pollution is leaving its mark on the trees and the parks.

Like most of the USSR's big cities, Moscow also seems to be located in the middle of the countryside. The urban districts come to a sudden halt on the edge of fields and forests, a virtue of Socialism, under which there is no land speculation, only the covetous and less damaging rivalry of neighboring administrations.

Soviet town planners have committed almost as many errors and created as many monstrosities as their counterparts in the West. However, Soviet cities lack the high-rise ugliness and overbuilt neighborhoods so typical of Western suburbia. Stalin and Khrushchev ordered the construction of elongated buildings, which are now surrounded by trees. Under Brezhnev, poorly built and poorly finished high-rise complexes with lots of space around them were erected. Today, they already look dilapidated.

THE CITY

The *taiga* is only a subway or bus ride away from the city since the countryside, some of it wild, some cultivated, lies just beyond Moscow's sixty-eight mile outer ring road. Elks wander freely a mere six miles from the Kremlin, and officials responsible for the Moscow National Park, a piece of wilderness tucked away in a corner of the city, have set up a brigade to rescue animals who wander into the dark streets bordering its 27,000 acres.

Legend has it that a few years ago a grey wolf lingered for several minutes near a bus shelter on the city limits before quietly returning to the forest nearby. It's a story told so many times that people aren't sure whether it's true or not.

In Moscow's parks a few thousand city residents, frustrated by the drudgery of urban living, have staked out private gardens to cultivate which no on dares dispute. Even at the foot of their massive residential complexes the Russians get back to their peasant roots, which can be found nearby. They never hesitate to replace a decorative tree with a fruit tree or a couple of raspberry bushes filched in the neighboring forest. This is Moscow village, with its wild strawberries, mushrooms, and flowers, where nature is still nature and not yet a greenbelt...

Like most other cities, Moscow is buried beneath snow for several months a year and gripped by the freezing cold for weeks on end. This is the time of year when towns and cities are transformed into playgrounds with toboggans and skis, when thousands of children skate on the smallest ponds or in the schoolyards sprayed with water as soon as the first frost sets in. It's a time when the cities' fur-hatted inhabitants refuse to yield to the harsh elements.

Moscow is like a magnet. Every day at least two million non-residents are drawn in, searching for products they can't find elsewhere. In every republic the capital cities attract such visitors, lengthening the lines in front of the stores. While the plan succeeds in distributing rare books that no one buys to rural areas, it fails to do the same for shoes, vacuum cleaners, and crockery.

In Moscow the crowds crisscross the city all day long, jumping on and off subway cars, buses, trolley buses, collective or individual taxis, which are cheap but, of course, never free at 6 p.m. At all hours these jostling masses, weighed down with bags and packages, converge on the subway, among the deepest in the world.

THE CITY

Soviet cities, like cities everywhere, lure people from the countryside and the distant republics. The population of Moscow has grown steadily and quite illegally, but with a regularity that shows that even the strictest regime is powerless in the face of modern urban trends. The capital should be limited to six million inhabitants, yet today it probably exceeds nine million, excluding the daily invasion of visitors looking for things to buy. Their perennial onslaught infuriates the Muscovites.

The cities bustle with bureaucrats, generating institution upon institution. They multiply, contradict each other and defend themselves with an energy born of despair. The constant abundance of white-collar workers contrasts sharply with the persistent shortage of manual labor. More than other cities, the capitals are infested with freeloaders because they are the centers of privilege and favoritism. Moscow, like St. Petersburg at the time of the tsars, is a glorious showcase, where everyone is tempted to help himself.

But it is also a schizophrenic city whose streets and neighborhoods range from the nineteenth to the twenty-first centuries, from glass buildings to battered industrial streets worthy of being classified as historic monuments. These streets from another age, with their factory and workshop courtyards, could serve as backdrops for old black and white movies.

THE CITY

LA VILLE

THE YUGO-ZAPAD DISTRICT IN MOSCOW

To the left of the residential blocks are the low buildings of the district school. After school, parents and children have access to the large school yard for walks and play. At the start of winter a school official floods the playground with water, which freezes in a matter of hours, to become a superb skating rink. It lasts all winter and only needs an occasional sweep to keep the snow off.

MOSCOW AT 22 BELOW ZERO

The Moskva River is frozen until early spring despite industrial effluence which makes the water a bit warmer. These superb plumes of smoke do not cause air polution, but are only clouds of vapor rising from a heating plant near the center of the city. Equipped with a town heating system, which also supplies hot water, Moscow never feels the cold.

103

THE CITY

AN OLD STREET IN TALLINN

The quiet streets of the historic center of Tallinn, capital of Estonia, are undergoing drastic change. The city authorities are encouraging people to reoccupy these moribund districts, where too many offices have been established. The proposed deal is simple: free rent in exchange for refurbishing apartments. Many people have left their houses or apartments in the suburbs to accept this challenge which could breathe new life into the center.

INNER COURTYARD IN TBILISI

This is not Naples but a typical inner courtyard in the center of Tbilisi, capital of Georgia.
The collective life here is due more to the southern atmosphere than to Socialism.
The exuberant Georgians have not yet given up the cult of "their" Stalin who was born in Gori, one of their small towns. It is the last republic where you can still ocassionally see his statue or bust.

THE CITY

EVERYDAY LIFE

Standing in line is part of the Soviet myth: tens of millions of people are always in search of the product that could appear at any moment, unexpectedly, before disappearing again for days or even years. The ways of the Plan are unfathomable, and every item leads a mysterious existence, usually quite unrelated to the needs of the consumer. It passed this way yesterday and tomorrow it will pop up somewhere else...

Everyday life consists of bags and packages, of searching and waiting, but also of unexpected little surprises like bumping into a store or a truck in the street with ripe strawberries or crates full of frozen chickens which can safely be unloaded in the snow at five degrees below zero.

In Moscow and the other big cities retail trading has taken to the streets. It's a never-ending lottery, with a superb surprise supper to win in a matter of minutes, or the ubiquitous *kapusta*, the cabbage used in each and every dish and in every imaginable way. "What's for supper tonight?" That's the unanswerable question of every housewife and her dear ones. They eat what's in the stores or what they can buy from a truck, and that's all there is to it.

"Guess who's coming to deliver tonight?" The towns and cities follow the pace of "commando teams," put together by the municipalities or private tradespeople to make up for the shortcomings of the flagging official distribution system. With or without humor, as the case may be, the Soviets are quite willing to explain to what extent consumerism is still a dream for them, but also an ever renewable feast. What a joy to find at last the rear-view mirror you've been seeking for months. What a delight to buy pantyhose that for once are not dark brown... So you buy up a good stock for the family, friends, friends of friends, and to pay the guy who comes to fix the kitchen stove when he's finished his official job. This is a country of scholar-plumbers, bureaucrat-carpenters and interpreter-plasterers, whose double lives earn them triple wages. This is a country where everyone is also someone else. Barter and exchanging services further reinforce the bustling community life, where the right address is not a hidden treasure but information to be exchanged... provided you return the favor, comrade.

People in the big cities cope by juggling with three distribution systems, which play hide and seek with customers and labels. The prices under the State system are unbeatable, but there is nothing quicker than popping down to the self-service store where "sales-artists" line up a few bottles and a couple of twin packs of something or other. In addition to these haphazard shopping expeditions, people can now go to the new, usually wellstocked cooperative stores mushrooming everywhere. Since the start of *perestroika* they, and particularly their prices, have caused quite an upheaval. Yet their prices never attain the heights of the more or less free market, where fruit, vegetables, meat, and poultry are usually in plentiful supply, particularly in summer. The same goes for flowers. Most Soviets are willing to spend their last rouble to buy flowers for someone, or for themselves, even in the midst of winter. Flowers are more than just decoration. They are a symbol, an offering. During the May 1st celebrations soldiers controlling the civilian parades buy them on Red Square from flower girls who miraculously escape all identity checks. Flower power, that's what it is.

The multiple distribution networks are among the new mysteries of Moscow and other cities, where items that never reach the State stores arrive in excellent condition in the stalls of private tradespeople. They are often the last link in a distribution chain which — from Georgia, Uzbekistan, Tadzhikistan or elsewhere — re-invented all those reviled agents and middlemen in the food business. In addition to the farmers who live near the big cities and sell their small, private output as it comes, there are now professional distributers. They get regular supplies or stay in town long enough to unload a truck or a railroad car, stocked over several thousand miles by various producers or cooperatives. The practice is illegal, but they do it openly. Some rent an apartment or buy one at an exorbitant price to have a drop-off point. Others arrange for a marriage of convenience with a Moscow girl so they can get a resident permit and do business in the capital. Business matchmaking is also a way of earning a living.

Strange relations are developing between the townsfolk and those slant-eyed merchants with their mat complexions… Racist remarks abound in those endless arguments about the high cost of cherries — seven roubles a kilo — in the middle of the cherry season. Buyers are fastidious in making their choices, checking out each stand. With such high prices they can't afford to make a mistake. Instead, many patiently wait for a surplus, which often leads to a sharp fall in prices, even below those in the cooperative shops. Walking through the market one quickly realizes that vendors have reached an agreement to maintain "coherent" prices for their products. The prices are high and, in theory, prohibitive for most shoppers. But theories hardly ever work in the USSR, and practice shows that these high prices penalize only a small segment of the population. In today's Soviet Union, with the bare necessities always provided for, the problem is not the lack of money, but more surprisingly, what to do with your money.

The "classified ads" section of the *Moscow Evening News* and the profusion of ads posted on outdoor bulletin boards are increasing evidence that the underground economy, no longer really clandestine, fulfills an essential, complementary function in society. In these ads apartments are offered for rent, sale, or exchange, as are automobiles, video recorders, fashionable bathing suits, television sets, cupboards, yoga manuals, exercise books by Jane Fonda or Raquel Welch, math lessons, bathroom faucets, and cassette tapes that sometimes go for as much as twenty roubles each. Like trading shares on the stock exchange, the price of every item fluctuates from day to day, depending on supply and demand. One day an entire bathroom ensemble went for the same price as ten blank cassette tapes…

There is, however, one product that was never in short supply under Brezhnev and has become a scarce commodity under the rigors of Gorbachev's reforms: vodka. The bottles that used to hide the empty spaces in many food stores have gone. The sale of vodka is now restricted to a limited number of stores from 2 p.m. to 7:30 p.m. This has prompted new, long, and meandering lines of thirsty Soviets, much to the exasperation of the policemen assigned to control them. The Soviets don't understand this change at all, even though it's explained to be in the interest of public health. In their apartments or in the back of their gardens they continue to distill millions of gallons of the traditional liquor, known as *samagon*. It's made from sugar snapped up from the stores, and almost anything they can lay their hands on. No amount of admonishing TV reports, newspaper articles, or speeches have any significant impact. From chic Party bosses to doddering grandmothers in headscarves, Soviets cheerfully carry on distilling their delicious and fearsome concoctions. Everyone does it, partly on principle, to defy the authorities who have ordained temperance.

The 64,000 rouble question is whether, all said and done, the Soviets are unhappy and dream of an advanced market economy that would spare them a life where they must engage in a daily quest for elusive products.

There is no answer to this misguided question, which implies that the Soviet Union is hell and the USA, for example, is paradise. A clear-cut answer would ignore the country's past, its cult of the bureaucracy, red tape, nitpicking identity checks, favoritism, and personal privilege. It's bureaucratic tradition has developed since the time of the tsars, when whole generations of generously remunerated pen-pushers devoured mountains of documents and permits.

Life isn't easy in Moscow, Leningrad, Minsk, and Kiev, nor in the hundreds of small provincial towns situated far away from the system's center. Yet, in their heart of hearts, many Soviets willingly concede that they don't want to abandon Socialism entirely. What they really want is both Socialism and capitalism. It's the eternal problem of wanting to have one's cake and eat it too...

EVERYDAY LIFE

EVERYDAY LIFE

MILK DELIVERY IN LENINGRAD

By organizing surprise sales like this the municipal authorities hope to put an end to the long lines caused by food shortages and the highly insufficient number of sales outlets. Moreover, Soviet town planners have scattered these outlets throughout the city following a logic that defies comprehension.

FLOWER GIRL IN MOSCOW

Muscovites buy and sell flowers in all seasons. Some flowers come from the south of the country, while others are grown in hothouses around the capital by ingeniously handy farmers who divert urban heating pipes for this purpose. At the end of winter, priced at two or three roubles for two or three flowers, flower growing is a profitable business.

EVERYDAY LIFE

PLUNGING VIEW OF GUM

The windows of this monumental and renowned Moscow department store overlook Red Square. Muscovites claim that most of the people making up the huge crowds constantly milling around several floors of immense galleries are out-of-towners and foreign tourists.
In theory everything is for sale in this department store, including snacks. In theory, of course... But a pleasant surprise can never be excluded.

PORCELAIN STORE IN LENINGRAD

This traditional porcelain, decorated with floral patterns, has been manufactured since the 18th century. It provides everything one needs for another tradition: tea. Even though the samovar has somewhat gone out of fashion, tea remains a genuine national drink in the Soviet Union, resulting in numerous ritual tea breaks.

EVERYDAY LIFE

EVERYDAY LIFE

EVERYDAY LIFE

AT THE COOPERATIVE MARKET IN MOSCOW

Opposite Riga Railroad Station in Moscow a huge "cooperative" market started in early 1987. Private craftsmen and traders sell gadgets, imitation American jeans, genuine T-shirts printed in English, shoes, belts, jewelry. In short, they sell things you often can't find in the shops, products which are, in most cases, better-made and more original. Babushkas also sell pre-war skirts and sweaters.

A FUNERAL IN TOWN

Religious burials are becoming more and more frequent, even for Party members. In many rural and some town churches, the dead lie in open coffins before the funeral ceremony begins. Families often organize funeral meals in church, according to Orthodox tradition.

EVERYDAY LIFE

FEMALE BRICKLAYERS

Many women work on construction sites in Moscow and Leningrad. The work may be difficult and exhausting, but it allows them to settle in these cities where residence is conditional on having a job. This measure was designed to prevent the disproportionate growth of the major cities. It proved to be a miscalculation because of people's resourcefulness and special favors to circumvent the rules, and the lack of labor in certain sectors. Once a residence permit has been stamped, a person can always look for another job…

116

EVERYDAY LIFE

EVERYDAY LIFE

EVERYDAY LIFE

STORE IN TALLINN SELLING EQUIPMENT FOR *DACHAS*

This store, selling furniture, fixtures, and fittings, is located in a region filled with many small country homes, known as *dachas*.
In Estonia and the other Baltic republics, despite the tyranny of the Plan, local business has often managed to adapt to demand. This is rare in Russia, where it usually takes years to change an old plan for supplies drawn up ages ago by some forgotten official.

COOPERATIVE STORE IN MOSCOW

To try to limit the success of private markets and, at the same time, remedy the notorious inadequacies of the State system, the authorities have encouraged the establishment of many cooperative stores. These stores sell the produce of the *kolkhozes*, big output or small, and the storekeepers may deal directly with them. This store in Petrovska Street in Moscow is one of those offering quality products.

MEAT DELIVERY

In winter the municipalities fight against the periodic and mysterious shortage of meat by arranging for deliveries by truck directly from cattle-breeding cooperatives.
At temperatures ranging from 5-20 below zero, refrigeration is no problem. So meat sold in the open air remains frozen. The choice is limited, but the Soviets do not share our traditional passion for steak.

EVERYDAY LIFE

STANDING IN LINE TO BUY VODKA

Vodka and wine are becoming more and more difficult to find, and people often have to wait patiently for hours before and after opening time (at 2 p.m.) at the few food stores, known as *produckty*, that still sell these items. Restrictive legislation introduced in 1985 has led to a sharp drop in alcohol consumption, according to the authorities. And there are a lot fewer drunks on the streets since this law, which severely punishes public drunkenness, was passed.

SALE OF *KVAS* IN THE STREET

Kvas is the national Russian drink. Made from fermented bread, this non-alcoholic beverage has its fanatic devotees and its staunch critics.
In fashionable society it's common to turn up one's nose at this folksy drink, with its undefinable taste reminiscent of cheap non-alcoholic beer. *Kvas* is sold in the street, and very rarely in cafes or food stores.

CLASSIFIED ADS, LENINGRAD STYLE

On the walls of the cities, to compensate for the lack of official advertising space, small personal ads are becoming more and more common. Some of these "billboards" are known for their real estaste ads.
Others specialize in offers for all kinds of lessons. Ads for all types of independant work, declared and otherwise, are publicly displayed.
In some cases, people in charge of businesses even place help wanted ads here. These panels, discreetly placed in the past, are mushrooming everywhere.

EVERYDAY LIFE

EVERYDAY LIFE

EVERYDAY LIFE

READING THE *MOSCOW NEWS*

Every Thursday the appearance of the *Moscow News* is a political event, eagerly awaited by Muscovites. The 500,000 copies printed in Russian are not enough to meet demand.

This ultra-Gorbachevian weekly, particularly hated by Party Conservatives, along with several others, has restored honor to the Soviet press. Those who can't get a copy make do with the foreign language edition or go to the newspaper's offices on Pushkin Square in central Moscow, where they can read the edition posted on the walls. Every week holds a few surprises for the readers of this topical paper.

IN THE SUBWAY

Even when newspapers were not so fascinating the Russians were voracious readers. Since the journalistic revolution at certain papers, readers have been devouring them. The Soviets read enormous amounts, wherever they happen to be and whatever their place in society.
The appearance of a new book is an event greeted with excitement by nearly everyone.

EVERYDAY LIFE

FLORIST'S STORE IN TALLINN

The traditional abacus has a prominent place in this store. From one end of the Soviet Union to the other it serves essentially to check calculations made on electronic cash registers. Older saleswomen are veritable virtuosos on the abacus, which is part of the country's commercial history.

SANDUNOVSKYE STEAM BATHS

Steam baths are still a very popular meeting place for Muscovites, but, of course, men and women don't share the same facilities. The Sandunovskye steam baths are among the oldest and best known in the capital. Women meet here to improve their figure, exchange the latest gossip, and discuss fashion or literature.

EVERYDAY LIFE

POLICE CONCERT IN THE CENTER OF MOSCOW

This traditional attraction appeals to fewer and fewer people and attendance has dropped considerably. Marching music is no longer fashionable, particularly in the big cities where rhythmic music has become popular.
All official entertainment is slowly losing favor.

LEISURE

With their relaxed attitude about working, the Soviets were probably the first to invent the leisure society. People talk about work. They make five-year plans and speeches about it. They develop statistics, graphs, books, films, heroes, medals, even large honor panels filled with retouched photographs to analyse and encourage it. But neither the Party nor the State is the taskmaster of the tsarist regime. Aleksey Stakhanov, the much-decorated Ukrainian miner of the 1930s who died several years ago as a bureaucrat in some government ministry, can rest in peace. His coal mining record will certainly never be broken and his name will live on in posterity as the man who developed the Stalinist work ethic, called *Stakhanovism*. Gorbachev's problem, however, is to convince his fellow countrymen to get down to work, not to teach them how to relax. They know how to goof off, and never fail to do so, even though this often means going on their interminable and not-so-relaxing shopping expeditions.

The Soviets go to work as little as possible. They have solved the unemployment problem by sharing the same job with others. This apparently is slated to change. No one believes it though. They do, however, believe that others should work a bit harder and a bit more often. Despite the Soviets' constant criticism of their compatriots' work habits, the country's trains, planes, subways, and buses do run on time, a reassuring paradox. Most people have debunked the work ethic so well that they have time to enjoy life.

One cliché about the Soviet Union is that it's a sad, drab place whose citizens are bored stiff because they can't play the races in the corner bar and are unhappy as can be with only five varieties of cheese, when they can get them. The reality is quite different. This is a country where people know how to cultivate the mind, make the best of life, laugh and have a good time. They don't need vodka to warm the heart and spirit. Russian conviviality is not just a myth, and it didn't disappear with Communism. In this country friends of friends are, indeed, friends. This is all the more true now that the suspicious attitudes of bleak and bygone years is beginning to fade.

Their joys are simpler and often more down-to-earth than ours. It's not just a question of choice or means. Going camping, for instance, is still an adventure rather than a temporary relocation of modern creature comforts. City residents are giving up group activities and vacations for the pleasure of rediscovering the countryside on their own. The demand for *dachas* (country homes) is so great that people have to go farther and farther away from town to obtain one. The weekend is gradually becoming an institution which empties the cities, even during the May 1st celebrations. It's a vital need rather than a social vogue. Concern about the environment is still very immediate and has not yet degenerated into a subject for political analysis.

Such outdoor pleasures are still the favorite pastimes of people who like to walk and exercise, in winter as well as summer. In the city jogging has become even more popular than in the West. In any case, the countryside is never far from people's thoughts.

Nowhere in the USSR do people take their leisure time for granted. There is no waste, especially in the cultural field, where there is still a lack of supply. Soviet citizens, whatever their station in life, read newspapers even more avidly than in the past, and despite three or four TV channels, they still devour books and like to go to the theater and the movies. There are never enough tickets to go around, but they will spend hours in line to get seats, which rarely cost more than two roubles each.

The Soviets are voracious readers. If Socialism achieves only one thing it will certainly be this zest for reading, this thirst for knowledge, this craving for the written word. For a long time Soviets were stuck with the worst types of printed material. Now that literary expression has been liberalized somewhat, they have the best. Their television churns out the same amount of inane programs that ours does, minus the game shows. Their shows have a lot of folk dancing, a little less accordion playing than in the past, tons of songs, rock music, and debates. TV debates and news programs are new phenomena and attract millions of TV viewers. They've never seen journalists or intellectuals exchanging views so frankly, or ministers and officials asked to "explain themselves". Almost equally fascinating are the commercials, which the kids adore, like kids everywhere.

Another simple joy is playing chess in the park for hours on end with chance acquaintances or friends. The game is so popular throughout the country that it has become a national sport, reported extensively on TV, with hours of running commentary when Grandmasters engage in battle.

Passions also run high during soccer and hockey games, rocking the stadiums in barely controllable waves during major matches. These days the authorities are more worried about sports matches than rock concerts. In addition to popular sports events, TV stations now regularly broadcast tennis matches and Formula-1 races, in response to the public's passion for individual distinction and cars.

Horse racing is another, less widely indulged passion, available in Moscow and a few other big cities. People eager to place bets run to and fro, between official betting counters and bookmakers, discreetly counting wads of roubles. The world of Soviet horse racing has always resisted puritanism and Socialist principles no matter what the race — gallop, trot, or in the winter, troika races. Since Gorbachev, betting is permitted not only on the lottery, but has been expanded to include all kinds of sports from chess tournaments to soccer and hockey matches.

If you add to all this the fact that the pet market is the most amazing place in Moscow, with people becoming increasingly attached to their dogs, or that the election of Miss Moscow in June 1988 proved a great success, you wonder what's the difference between them and us?

LEISURE

LEISURE

STREET ARTIST IN ARBAT STREET

In the spring of 1987 over one hundred painters and caricaturists took over Arbat Street, the pedestrian street in Moscow, which has become a kind of permanent art and music show. It's a far cry from the promenade city planners envisaged before Gorbachev-style liberalism engulfed the city. As everywhere, local residents are beginning to complain.

BOOKSELLER ON ARBAT STREET

Many small businesses have sprung up on this street, in addition to the activities of the painters and musicians. On some days there are even rare book merchants, selling books for over 250 roubles each. That's the equivalent of an unskilled worker's monthly wages in Moscow. Yet, it's easy to find collectors for these treasures.

LEISURE

MUCH-DECORATED DOG

At Moscow's bird market one finds all kinds of animals, from chickens to goldfish. But more and more people are buying cats and especially dogs. Dogs with a pedigree, or those who have won prizes in contests, sell for a lot of money. It's not surprising, therefore, that they have begun to invade the streets and parks. Canned dog food, though, is still non-existent.

WINTER CHESS GAME

This national sport knows neither season nor rest, and is practiced by millions of Soviets in all the republics. Major contests at home and abroad are regularly broadcast on television with lively commentary. There are chess journals and chess clubs, and the game is at least as important as soccer or hockey. In the parks certain players don't hesitate to play for money.

LEISURE

LEISURE

134

LEISURE

WINTER DIP IN THE NEVA

The "Walruses" of Moscow and Leningrad enjoy a dip in the freezing waters of the Neva River. Every winter enthusiasts of this icy dip, which can last only about 30 seconds, get together opposite the Peter Paul Fortress in Leningrad. They dig a trench in the icy river which they keep open throughout winter. The most fanatical of these bathing aficionados even get children to take part in their adventure.

Now that the newspapers and television can examine almost any trivial subject without reference to Marx or Lenin, there are serious discussions about the pros and cons of such practices. Nevertheless, there are always far more spectators than participants, grateful for the towels proffered by these helpful, but not-so-daring, bystanders; they don't even take their gloves off. Of course, the temperature during these immersions hovers around 11 degrees below zero. The flippers serve to keep their feet from freezing.

LEISURE

LEISURE

FISHING ON THE FROZEN NEVA

Fishing in wintertime is a very popular sport in Leningrad. All one has to do is drill a hole in the Neva, wait, and pull up. The fish at the end of the line is frozen in a matter of minutes. The most obstinate fishermen, those who remain immobile for hours in glacial temperatures, must take certain precautions to avoid being frozen before their catch. Some people also go ice fishing at sea. During the springtime a few of them unthinkingly wander too far from the coast… floating off into the sea on a chunk of ice that has become detached. In 1986 helicopters had to bring back several reckless adventurers from a small floe that had broken off and drifted offshore. Such cases are quite frequent and rescuers have noted that many of those brought back to shore had imbibed considerable quantities of alcohol… as antifreeze, of course.

LEISURE

IN GORKY PARK

On the banks of the Moskva River, still largely free of traffic, Moscow's Gorky Park offers its benches to strollers and its footpaths to joggers.
The park is also the site of the annual war veterans' meeting. On May 9th, anniversary of the victory marking the end of the war in 1945, the former soldiers mill around placards identifying their old regiments. Sometimes, in this way, they find comrades-in-arms they have not seen for over 40 years.

MOSCOW BIRD MARKET

The bird market near Taganka Street, which started some 30 years ago, attracts more and more people. Since business is flourishing — from the sale of the family kitten, to unloading blue-fish, worms, bird-seed, or dog breeding products — it's becoming more and more difficult to find an empty spot to set up shop.

SOCCER MATCH UNDER SURVEILLANCE

Major soccer matches in Moscow are getting rowdier all the time, and the authorities have had to take measures to avoid overcrowding and to avoid placing rival fan clubs in the same bleachers.
On several occasions fans of the Spartak team from Moscow caused trouble for the police by attacking the homebound buses and trains of fans of a rival team.

138

LEISURE

LEISURE

AT THE MOSCOW RACETRACKS

The Moscow racetracks have virtually never stopped operating, even in the darkest years under Stalin. In fact, Stalin had part of the complex rebuilt to give it a more monumental appearance. An extraordinary crowd gathers here several times a week to place their bets. In winter amazing troika races are held on which major bets can be placed. Betting is officially controlled, but there are a couple of successful bookmakers who tend to ignore the impassive gaze of the policemen on duty.

140

LEISURE

CHECKROOM PAINTING

Off-track betting is illegal in Moscow. Even so, betting often takes place through neighborhood bookmakers. Triple races or simple races are not broadcast on television. In general, betters are not just amateurs trying to make a few roubles but fanatics convinced they have the best tips. The take on certain races can exceed a thousand roubles, so they can win considerable sums... if they're lucky.

DRYING MEAT IN KIRGIZIA

This woman of Mongol origin, a large community in this republic, will take several days to prepare and smoke her beef and goat meat.
It can be easily stored all winter, serving to feed the family and the shepherds tending the flocks on the road.

THE EXOTIC EMPIRE

When Natasha prepares breakfast in Smolensk, in the west of the country, her brother Pyotr sits down for supper in Vladivostok, on the Pacific coast. It takes just as long to fly across the Soviet Union as it takes to fly from Moscow to New York. Grasping the immensity of the Soviet Union is one of the keys to understanding the country. It stretches over six thousand miles from west to east and some three thousand miles from north to south. The tsars built an empire which the Soviets proceeded to expand, somewhat like one expands a flourishing family business. In this case the family is Russian, and their 140 million members continue unabashedly their centuries-old domination of the hundred other ethnic nationalities scattered across the empire. These peoples speak Russian more or less willingly but, once they leave school, are quite happy to forget the imposing language of Mother Russia.

To ask whether the Soviets want to leave their country is to forget how immense it is and how strongly they feel attached to it, leaving aside the possible attractions of our exotic Western society. In one country they find what we must travel elsewhere to see: the rough charms of the polar circle, inhabited by roaming reindeer; the languidness of the Caspian Sea, situated at the same latitude as Majorca; the Germanic flavor of Tallinn and Riga, or the oriental ambience of Dushambe and Bukhara. There is the inescapable and monotonous taiga, the tundra, the marshes and moors of Siberia, where the soil never thaws deeper than three feet, the rambling mountains of the Caucasus and the sheer slopes of the Pamir range, where shepherds dream and wander as in the past, eternal nomads in spite of all the changes. For centuries the ruling Russians sought a miraculous synthesis between the lumberjacks of Pskov, the grape-pickers of Georgia, and the sheep breeders of Turkmenia, between the cold and the heat, and between the tall blonds and the short, dark-skinned peoples who live and die in different worlds. All countries have an east and a west, but in the Soviet Union the east is Asia and the west is Europe. Moreover, the country has unparalleled natural resources. Above ground everything grows in abundance; underground there are reserves for centuries to come.

As a multiracial State the Soviet Union has inherited the delicate balance envisaged by the tsars. It is based on the following principle: "Everyone has a homeland somewhere and the Russians have a homeland everywhere." While other nationalities rarely leave their own republics or autonomous regions, the Russians are all over the country, guaranteeing the reality of Soviet unity and the veneer of Soviet uniformity. They Russify everything and become the majority group wherever it is politically or economically necessary and feasible. Take, for example, Uzbekistan and the Ukraine. The former has fantastic mining resources and an impressive textile industry, the latter is the country's wheat belt; both of fundamental importance to national security. But Uzbekistan can't claim the same independence as the Ukraine which, most people forget, is represented at the United Nations. Therefore, when Ukrainians protested to Soviet authorities after the Chernobyl nuclear disaster, they were promised that no more nuclear plants would be built in their republic.

The Soviet Union is an exotic land, filled with contrast and awesome images. I often think about the first time I saw the Siberian town of Irkutsk or the first night I heard the roar of the Angara River. The images are entangled with all that I've read and dreamed about the Soviet Union... of Michel Strogoff, the Jules Verne character, stranded on an ice floe in the Siberian capital, besieged by hordes of barbarians. The sun is about to rise in this oft-imagined Siberia. It comes up over the Angara, that mighty river born of three hundred and sixty-five brooks and streams feeding into Lake Baikal. On the other side of the river weaves the Trans-Siberian Railroad, spitting steam from every wagon.

The first train arrived on the banks of the Angara in 1898. Today there is one every ten minutes... Near the river stands a train station caravansary, with several clocks which have been indicating the time in all parts of the empire for the past hundred years. Beneath the clocks travellers wait for the train — Georgians, Tadzhiks, Uzbeks, Turkmenians, Buryats, Yakuts, or Uighurs. They can also be found in Moscow's huge Kazan Station, with their suitcases, packages, bundles and kettles. This exoticism and tumult is the gateway to the USSR's Orient.

Siberia has always thrilled the Russians' imagination; they embarked on several grandiose projects in an effort to dominate the wild and vast region. Their efforts were not always successful. In one project, aimed at settling the inhospitable regions of the province, they built an 1,800 mile branch of the Trans-Siberian Railroad, which remains inoperable today. In another project, aimed at providing water to the south, planning officials wanted to reroute the course of several great Siberian rivers from their natural outlet in the Polar seas to the south. With the arrival of Gorbachev, however, scientists and environmentalists blocked the plan, which would have devastated Siberia and its climate. It was a mad, herculean project, commensurate to the magnitude of the country and its dreams of domination.

For more exoticism and more contrast there is Riga, the old city, and Tallinn, the ancient city, each capital of a republic that is increasingly turning its back on Russia. In July 1988, in Tukums, some thirty-five miles from Riga, a ten-year-old girl scolded a grocery store clerk for answering her only in Russian. Emotions ran high in the store, with all the Latvians present approving this juvenile revolt. In the coastal villages, set among the fragrant pine and myrtle trees, people easily forget Russian and speak it brokenly when they have to. This happens in Uzbekistan, in the Georgian hamlets celebrating the grape harvest, and even in certain ministries, a fact that provokes a lot of laughter... among the Russians of course...

While some exotic traits irritate the Russians, others don't. Long ago the Georgians transformed their republic into a private business. This has allowed them to make a fortune in the illicit fruits and vegetables trade which, however, saves Moscow, Kiev, Leningrad and several other cities from food shortages. The Uzbeks, on the other hand, haven't had such luck. Under Brezhnev they tranformed their local Communist

Party into a veritable mafia. But an examining magistrate and a hundred investigators have been filing charges relentlessly since 1986 and crowding the prisons with hapless Uzbeks, discovered with hidden roubles, gold, and jewelry. The new "market agents" thriving under Gorbachev also rankle the Russians. Generally from the south, they openly took over much of the country's food distribution activities from a State incapable of efficiently organizing them. Most irksome is that these nouveaux riches come to White Russia to spend their money, unconsciously flaunting their roubles wherever they wine and dine.

There is also exoticism in the two craggy-faced men from Bukhara, talking for hours on the patio of a cafe in the center of town about the *kalim* (the dowry) to be paid before the marriage of the daughter of one with the son of the other. Over glasses of mint tea their discussion goes on forever. Before the date is fixed for Friday at the mosque, they agree on a sum of several thousand roubles. The two fathers, big carpet manufacturers and sheepherders, have considerable property in this oasis town. The practice of *kalim* is so widespread here that the Moscow newspapers denounced it in 1987. It made no difference, however. Not many Bukharans are avid readers of national dailies. Moscow is at the end of the world for many Soviet cities, despite all the streets named after Marx, Frunze, the Communards, the 40th Anniversary of October, and, of course, Lenin. Only Brezhnev Street has recently disappeared in many towns...

Exoticism has its conflict. The world expected the revolt of the Uzbeks, Azerbaijanis, Tatars, Kazakhs, Tadzhiks, Turkmenians, Kirghiz, Chuvash, Bashkirs, Chechen, Udmurts, Ossetes, Buryats, Yakuts, Balkars, or Kalmyks against the Russians. The Armenian conflict reminds us that the fiercest antagonism erupts first between peoples obliged to live together and interact in a multitude of republics, regions, or autonomous territories.

In simple terms, the protracted Armenian conflict is not much more — though this is enormous in itself — than the explosion of centuries of hatred between Christians of the Armenian Orthodox rite and Shiite Muslims, long exposed to religious propaganda from Iran. The Nagorno-Karabakh autonomous region in revolt is a Christian enclave in a Muslim world. For decades the fuse had been smoldering slowly, with claims and tension that never came out into the open.

The massacre of dozens of Armenians in Sumgait, on the Caspian Sea, was an expression of an old Azerbaijani hatred, a demon which the local authorities have never managed to quash. Only the Soviet Army, under orders from Moscow, came to the rescue of the beleaguered Armenians, preventing further widespread casualties. The Russians, therefore, pose no problems to the Armenians. Only about ten percent of the population of Armenia is Russian, and mixed marriages are among the rarest in the country. It's the Azerbaijanis who are the enemy. And the feeling is mutual.

In many regions minor or major nationalities find the indiscriminate intermingling imposed by the tsars, Stalin, and historical coincidence hard to bear. The result is friction that could erupt into civil war. The Soviet authorities recognize that in about twenty hot spots throughout the country the situation is potentially explosive. Open struggle would have a disrupting effect on the economy, as it did for months in Armenia. However, all these parallel conflicts don't preclude the eventual rejection of the Russians, those old scapegoats, so convenient and necessary...

The USSR is not only a patchwork, it's also a marvelous mosaic, which even includes a Jewish region, Birobidzhan. Twenty thousand Jews, voluntary exiles and settlers, live in this distant corner of eastern Siberia. It was created in 1934, with Yiddish as the official language. The Jews there constitute only a fraction of the Soviet Union's Jewish population, which totals about two million, according to census results. In the USSR every citizen, in addition to his Soviet citizenship, is also a Jew, a Tatar, Moldavian, Byelorussian, Lithuanian, Kazakh, or Russian. Being Jewish, therefore, is a nationality like any other, or almost...

Moscow, Leningrad, and Kiev are stirring while the rest of the empire moves imperceptibly. The shock waves caused by Gorbachev may well take years to reach the outer reaches of the Soviet world. It's a world that has always believed that immobility is superior to movement, whether it goes by the name of Revolution, *glasnost*, or *perestroika*.

THE EXOTIC EMPIRE

FANCY DRESS...

For the October crop and grape harvest festivals that take place in Tbilisi and many other Georgian towns, men dress up as the female characters of the regional folk theater.

This one-day festival is an extraordinary event of joy, drinking, and excesses of all kinds. The police avoid getting involved and decline to keep the ever-growing crowd in order.

... FOR THE HARVEST FESTIVAL IN TBILISI

The Russian veneer of the Georgians comes off rather quickly, especially after a lot of wine, cognac, and vodka. At such times they invoke Stalin and call the Russians all sorts of names. But the fact remains that this great festival, held at the end of summer, shows that the exuberant Georgians know how to have a good time — a far cry from the stuffy official celebrations held elsewhere in the country.

THE EXOTIC EMPIRE

THE EXOTIC EMPIRE

MONGOL WOMAN OF KIRGIZIA

This woman, from a Central Asian republic incorporated into the Russian Empire at the end of the 19th century, has preserved a completely traditional way of life. Like the patchwork in the background, the Soviet Union is comprised of hundreds of nationalities, each distinct but forming one entity.

A GOAT SACRIFICED IN HONOR OF A VISITOR

The economy of the mountainous Kirkizia region bordering China is still based on traditional sheepherding. The wealth of the local shepherds is measured by the size of their flocks. This doesn't stop them, however, from sacrificing an animal for a visiting guest.

THE EXOTIC EMPIRE

SEAL HUNTER ON THE SAKHALIN PENINSULA

This strategically important region, the Far East of the Soviet Union, remains formally forbidden to foreigners. The seal fishermen and hunters of Nivkh origin lead a very traditional life in this superb area on the Pacific shore.
Seal meat and fish are dried or pickled to be sold on the market or to ships who drop anchor in the port.

KOREAN FAMILY

There are many Soviets of Korean origin living on the Sakhalin Peninsula. Some of the country's 400,000 Koreans have kept their original nationality, a kind of stigma which neither facilitates their lives nor their travels, even though Korean is one of the country's official languages. This young woman, like many of her compatriots, works in a fish-canning plant, one of the region's main economic activities.

RUSSIAN FISHERMAN OF SAKHALIN

In this region, first colonized long ago when the tsars still owned Alaska, there are also Russian fishermen. Their means of subsistence and their fishing methods are no different from those of the other peoples of the region.

THE EXOTIC EMPIRE

THE EXOTIC EMPIRE

STORE WINDOW IN TALLINN

In Tallinn, Estonian — a language similar to Finnish — is as important as Russian. The Estonians in this westward-looking Baltic capital are lucky to be able to receive Western TV programs from Sweden or Finland. And they don't deprive themselves. They have long been charmed by life in "Dallas", and some teenagers are still fascinated by it. Arriving in this city, Russian travellers have the impression of beginning to leave the USSR...

THE EXOTIC EMPIRE

ON THE SHORES OF THE BALTIC

Tallinn is an old city facing the sea. Its yachting club, built for the 1980 Olympics, is one of the most active and classiest in the entire country. Tallinn invented private restaurants well before the Law of 1987, and its inhabitants have even managed to lend some charm to certain State enterprises, like this restaurant on the coast where the food is very good.

THE EXOTIC EMPIRE

THE MINES OF VORKUTA

These infamous mines, at the freezing cold end of the Urals, were set up by Stalin as internment and hard labor camps. Conditions were worsened by temperatures often reaching 40 below for weeks on end during the winter, when the sun hardly rises above the horizon. The camps have gone, but the cold remains. In 1988 the government decided to erect a monument here to the victims of Stalin.

THE EXOTIC EMPIRE

RED FLAG IN MOURNING

Here, in a hamlet in Vorkuta in the dead of winter, lies a powerful memory, image, and symbol of life to come: the black ribbon attached to the red flag marks the death of Leonid Brezhnev announced that morning. Yet in this frozen desert, where daylight hardly penetrates, the blizzard rages on, and no one is aware that one day a powerful thaw will set in.

LANDMARKS

HISTORIC LANDMARKS

988 Having recently come under the firm rule of Scandinavian Princes, the Slavs convert to Christianity.

1200-1300 Tatars gradually invade Russian territory, settling along the Volga River.

1236-1263 Reign of Alexander Nevsky, grand prince of Vladimir, who helped transform Russia into a state.

1499 Ivan III expands Russia to the Urals.

1533-1584 Reign of Ivan IV, known as Ivan the Terrible, who was the first to bear the title of Tsar. Start of Russian expansion into Siberia.

1610 The Cossacks reach the Yenisey River, which becomes the frontier of Russia in 1619.

1682-1725 Reign of Peter I, known as Peter the Great. He transfers the capital to St. Petersburg (now Leningrad).

1762-1796 Reign of Catherine II, known as Catherine the Great. Russia expands to the Black Sea.

1855-1881 Reign of Alexander II, the tsar who abolished serfdom in 1861 and was later assassinated. Expansion throughout the 19th century to central Asia (Tadzhikistan, Kazakhstan, Turkmenistan, Turkistan, Kirgizia) and eastern Asia (provinces of the Amur, Maritime province, Sakhalin).

1891-1904 Building of the Trans-Siberian railroad.

1904-1905 War between Russia and Japan.

1905 First Russian revolution. The army fires on people marching under the priest Gapon. Mutiny on the battleship Potemkin in Odessa.

October 25th, 1917 Siege of the Winter Palace and start of the October Revolution (celebrated on November 8th because at the time the Russians still used the old Orthodox calendar).

December 30th, 1922 Creation of the Union of Soviet Socialist Republics by the First Congress of Soviets.

January 21st, 1924 Death of Vladimir Ilich Ulyanov, known as Lenin.

1927 Stalin victorious in the struggle with Trotsky and Zinovyev, who where expelled from the Party.

1929 Collectivization of agriculture begins.

1936-38 Stalin's great purge. Moscow trials.

August 23rd, 1939 Signing of German-Soviet non-aggression pact.

June 22nd, 1941 USSR attacked by Germany.

March 5th, 1953 Death of Stalin.

February 14th-25th, 1956 Twentieth Communist Party Congress and first attempt at de-Stalinization.

October 14th, 1964 Nikita Khrushchev deposed "for health reasons".

August 1975 Final Act of the Helsinki Conference on the Free Flow of Men and Ideas.

October 7th, 1977 Adoption of a new constitution. Brezhnev in the Presidium of the Supreme Soviet.

November 10th, 1982 Death of Brezhnev. He had gradually accumulated all power in the Party and the State apparatus.

March 13th, 1985 Mikhail Sergeyevitsh Gorbachev elected to the post of General Secretary of the Communist Party by the Politiburo, with a majority of only one vote according to political rumor.

May 1st, 1987 Promulgation of the law permitting individual and family private enterprises.

LANDMARKS TODAY

- The Union of Soviet Socialist Republics covers an area of 8,650,000 square miles with a total population of 284 million. It encompasses 15 federated republics: Russia, the Ukraine, Byelorussia, Armenia, Azerbaidzhan, Georgia, Turkmenistan, Uzbekistan, Tadzhikistan, Kazakhstan, Kirghiz, Estonia, Lithuania, Latvia and Moldavia.
- The federated republics encompass 20 other autonomous republics and eight autonomous regions.
- The constitution of the USSR recognizes about 100 nationalities, some of which have only a few thousand members.
- 130 languages using five different alphabets are spoken on USSR territory.
- The Russian Soviet Federated Socialist Republic is the largest of the republics. It extends to the Pacific and has a total area of 6,592,800 square miles with 145 million inhabitants.
- The smallest of the federated republics is Estonia with 17,400 square miles and 1,300,000 inhabitants.
- Siberia has an area of 2,340,000 square miles, of which 1,560,000 never thaw beyond a depth of five feet (the temperature drops to ninety below zero). Winter may last for 6-8 months.
- In the extreme south of Soviet Asia the desert of Kara-Kum or the Kyzyl-Kum Desert may reach temperatures of 140 Fahrenheit.
- Soviet television viewers get four channels (two national channels, a regional channel and a cultural educational channel).
- There are 8,400 newspapers with a combined total of 43.2 billion copies printed each year. The newspaper with the largest circulation is *Trud*, the trade union paper printing 18.5 million copies a year. Pravda has a total annual circulation of 11 million.
- The Soviet currency unit is the rouble.

Victoria Ivleva wishes to thank

the Amossov family, Nikita Antonov, Rimma Bagatova, Alexander Bakharevsky, Tatiana Divakova, Eleonora, Sergey Golubkov, the Kozhayev family, Elena Kosarzhevskaya, Nastya and Vera Kravstov, Alla Krivotsheyna, Sergey Matusov, Leonid Morgunov, Anna Neistat, Vladimir Saytsev, Valeria and Dasha Salivako, Elena Skvortsova, Leonid Valeyev, Dimitri Voltshek, Alla Yakobson, Victoria Zaytshik.

She is especially indebted to her parents.